Peasants Wake for Fellini's *Casanova* and Other Poems

Peasants Wake for Fellini's *Casanova*

and Other Poems

Andrea Zanzotto

Edited and
Translated by
John P. Welle
and
Ruth Feldman

Drawings by
Federico Fellini
and
Augusto Murer

University of Illinois Press Urbana, Chicago & Springfield

Publication of this book was supported by a grant from the Institute for Scholarship in the Liberal Arts, College of Arts and Letters, University of Notre Dame.

Manufactured in the United States of America
1 2 3 4 5 C P 6 5 4 3 2

This book is printed on acid-free paper.

Drawings used with permission of the late Federico Fellini and the heirs of Augusto Murer.

Selected poems from *Filò per il Casanova di Fellini* (1988) and *Idioma* (1986) appear in the original Italian courtesy of Arnoldo Mondadori Editore S.p.A.

Jacket drawing by Angelina Sari used with permission of the artist.

Library of Congress Cataloging-in-Publication Data

Zanzotto, Andrea, 1921–
[Poems. English. Selections]
Peasants wake for Fellini's Casanova and other poems / Andrea Zanzotto ; edited and translated by John P. Welle and Ruth Feldman ; drawings by Federico Fellini and Augusto Murer.
p. cm.
Selected poems from the author's Filò and Idioma appear in the original Italian.
ISBN 978-0-252-02310-1 (cloth : alk. paper). — ISBN 978-0-252-06610-8 (paper : alk. paper)
I. Welle, John P., 1951– . II. Feldman, Ruth. III. Title.
PQ4851.A74A28 1997
851'.914—dc20 96-31442
CIP

Contents

Introduction John P. Welle

"And now I have to dub it, this film which I have shot recklessly in English, and among the many problems there is also that of the Veneto dialect." In this way, Federico Fellini begins his letter to Andrea Zanzotto, inviting the poet to write the dialogue in a pseudo-Venetian dialect from the eighteenth century, partly invented, partly imitated, for two of the scenes for his movie *Casanova* (1976). Zanzotto not only collaborated with the filmmaker on this occasion but was also involved in two subsequent Fellini films, *La città delle donne* (The City of Women, 1980) and *E la nave va* (And the Ship Sails On, 1983). More important, however, the challenge of inventing poetic texts in Venetian dialect to accompany Fellini's visual evocations of two female figures—the woman's head rising from the lagoon in the first scene of the film, and, in a later scene, the giantess from the Veneto who sings a plaintive lullaby—stimulated Zanzotto to enter into a whole new phase of poetic experimentation of his own.

In response to the film, and to the erasure of the centuries-old peasant civilization centered in orality, Zanzotto composed a third text: "Filò," whose English title, "Peasants Wake," was suggested by the poet himself in homage to James Joyce's *Finnegans Wake*. An elegy in dialect on the continual death and resurgence of the dialects, "Peasants Wake" stages a dialogue between poetry and film, between the spoken idiom of a small agricultural community and the brave new visual language of an increasingly global society. Zanzotto's book *Filò per il Casanova di Fellini* (Peasants Wake for Fellini's *Casanova*, 1976), translated here into English for the first time and presented in a multilingual format, was born from that encounter between Italy's most innovative living poet and one of her most brilliant filmmakers. Described by the critic Gianfranco Contini as "one of the most singular contributions to the repertoire of Italian dialect literature," "Peasants Wake" constitutes the first in a series of poetic explorations by Zanzotto in the vanishing mother tongue(s) of his native region.

Peasants Wake for Fellini's Casanova *and Other Poems* not only makes available in English the poetic results of Zanzotto's collaboration with Fellini but adds to that unique work a compendium of his dialect poetry that followed, along with a modest, thematically cohesive selection of his poetry in Italian from the late 1970s until today. The majority of the Italian poems presented here, as well as all of the dialect poems after *Peasants Wake for Fellini's* Casanova, stem from *Idioma* (Idiom, 1986), the third book in a trilogy—or "pseudo-trilogy," according to the poet—consisting of *Il Galateo in Bosco* (The Book of Forest Manners, 1978) and *Fosfeni* (Phosphenes, 1983, a title that refers to the small points of light seen behind closed eyelids when rubbing them). Gian Luigi Beccaria has called Zanzotto's trilogy "one of the most coherent and significant linguistic and poetic experiments in twentieth-century Italian literature." *Idioma,* the volume from which the second part of this book derives, contains a mixture of poems in Italian and in Solighese dialect. It focuses primarily on the people and the daily reality of Zanzotto's native village, Pieve di Soligo. The concentrated use of dialect is fitting, therefore, because the inhabitants of this small community form their identities, express themselves, and communicate in a common idiom that for Zanzotto still "contains a drop of Eve's milk."

Born in Pieve di Soligo on October 10, 1921, Andrea Zanzotto earned a degree in letters from the University of Padua in 1942 and took part in the Resistance. Following the conclusion of hostilities, he spent two years working in France and Switzerland and later returned to his native town, where he has been a teacher and administrator for over forty years and where he currently resides. Eugenio Montale, winner of the Nobel Prize for Literature in 1975, christened Zanzotto "the most important Italian poet born in this century." Montale, of course, was himself born in the final years of the previous century. It was also Montale who noted that Zanzotto's poetry expresses the tragic discord between what Christians call "the soul" and scientists term "the psyche." Zanzotto's poetry explores the self, the links between nature and culture, and the origins of poetry and myth. His work is informed by the main currents of modern and postmodern European thought: the philosophy of Martin Heidegger, the linguistics of Roman Jakobson, the psychoanalysis of Jacques Lacan, as well as scientific theories and discoveries. With the volumes of his middle period—*La Beltà* (Beauty, 1968) and *Pasque* (Easters, 1973)—Zanzotto begins to create poetry intended as a form of resistance, however marginalized, to the abusive power of history. Constructed to express a plurality of meaning, his poetry is highly self-referential, hermetic, and intellectually challenging: qualities that have led some critics to consider his work excessively difficult and even impenetrable at times. While his verse attempts to combine the analytic and the elegiac, Zanzotto, in the dialect phase privileged in this volume, clearly adopts the traditional stance of the poet as commemorator.

Zanzotto's career spans five decades and has been marked by dramatic stylistic turns while remaining faithful to a central core of thematic issues. Together with such writers and poets of his generation as Italo Calvino, Pier Paolo Pasolini, and Paolo Volponi, Zanzotto expresses the trauma that Italy has undergone in the transformation from a rural, chiefly agricultural and traditional society to one of the most highly industrialized countries in the West. The lyrical celebration of nature in his early poetry turned into mourning its despoilment in the 1960s and 1970s. He has published fourteen volumes of poetry to date, for which he has won major literary prizes including the Saint-Vincent Prize in 1950, the Viareggio Prize in 1978, the Eugenio Montale–Librex Prize in 1983, and the Accademia dei Lincei Prize in 1987. Most recently, the German city of Münster awarded him its coveted European Poetry Prize. He has also published two prose works, two volumes of literary criticism, and has translated such French writers as Balzac, Michaux, Bataille, and Leiris. Zanzotto himself has been widely translated into French and enjoys a considerable following among French intellectuals.

In 1996, Zanzotto brought out a new collection of poetry, *Meteo* (Donzelli Editore), with drawings by Giosetta Fioroni. The title, which refers to meteorological phenomena, reflects the language of Italian television. Weather broadcasts in current journalistic jargon are known as *meteo.* Consisting of some twenty poems written in the decade after *Idioma,* Zanzotto's *Meteo* offers a succinct preview of a larger work-in-progress. In the "New Poems" section of *Peasants Wake for Fellini's* Casanova *and Other Poems,* we provide two texts—both highly topical, like the majority of the poems in *Meteo*—from Zanzotto's most recently published book. "Ticking (Like a Geiger Counter)" explores the consequences of the Chernobyl nuclear disaster, and "Other Poppies" treats the war in Bosnia.

Unlike his contemporaries in the immediate post–World War II period who were moving away from hermeticism and symbolism toward more explicitly realist and "engaged" forms of writing, Zanzotto lingered within the earlier modes and developed them in a personal fashion. In discussing his early work, critics often emphasize influences and affinities with such poets as Hölderlin, Rilke, Lorca, Eluard, Leopardi, and Ungaretti, and with the hermeticism of Luzi. While Zanzotto evolves from within hermeticism, his work has always been marked by experimental energy, intellectual depth, and a conscious attempt to renew the Italian poetic tradition.

The books of Zanzotto's early period, consisting of *Dietro il paesaggio* (Behind the Landscape, 1951), *Elegia e altri versi* (Elegy and Other Verses, 1954), *Vocativo* (Vocative, 1957), and *IX Ecloghe* (IX Eclogues, 1962), capture the pastoral beauty of the rolling hills and snowy peaks of the northern Veneto: a verdant landscape rendered tragic by two world wars. They also explore the self while making use of traditional Italian poetic forms, vocabulary, and motifs. The titles of his early works indicate the psychological direction in his work: his is an increasingly self-referential poetry drawing upon the elegy, the Latin vocative case, and the eclogue. In *IX Eclogues,* the closing book of his first period, Zanzotto expands his poetic diction beyond its Petrarchan and symbolist base to embrace the most recent scientific and technological vocabularies. In this way, the evolution of Zanzotto's poetry in the late fifties and early sixties reflects the concurrent move toward metalanguage in avant-garde letters, literary criticism, and the human sciences. Although at the close of his early phase Zanzotto had not yet begun to publish poetry in his native dialect, we find him already reflecting on its disappearance: "Pace per me, per voi / buona gente senza più dialetto" (Peace to me, to you / good people who no longer possess a dialect).

La Beltà intensifies the metalinguistic and metapoetic tendencies of Zanzotto's previous work and marks a watershed in his development. Regarded as one of the most innovative poetic achievements of the postwar period, Zanzotto's experimental lyrics fracture the tenuous bond linking the signifier to the signified. Language itself becomes the subject of Zanzotto's discourse in the books of his middle period through an exaggerated alliteration, a Joycean wordplay, and the manipulation of morphological elements. Moreover, *La Beltà* mirrors the anger, frustration, and disorientation of the 1960s, a time that saw tremendous social upheaval in Italy, as well as the disappearance of traditional peasant customs. This volume also contains the famous "Elegia in petèl" (Elegy in Baby-Talk), to which Fellini refers in his letter to Zanzotto included here.

In 1969 Zanzotto published *Gli sguardi i fatti e senhal* (Gazes Facts and Senhal), a long poem modeled on the Rorschach test, which treats the television coverage of the American lunar landing as a shredding of the mythic fabric that once surrounded the moon in the popular imagination. In *Pasque* Zanzotto plays on the etymology of *pasqua,* a word in Hebrew and in Latin meaning "passage" and "pasture," respectively. One of his most challenging and enigmatic works, this volume complements and develops the iconoclastic energy of *La Beltà.* Easters, which never occur, constitute metaphorical "Passovers" and "passages" from one state of being to another: potentially liberating experiences, these desired transformations remain blocked today, primarily by a rapacious consumer capitalism and by the stultifying conventions of formal schooling and organized religion.

As indicated at the outset, in the phase of experimentation whose trajectory begins with the Fellini collaboration and extends through *Idioma,* Zanzotto turns increasingly to the dialects of his native region. Together with such poets as Pier Paolo Pasolini, Tonino Guerra, Amedeo Giacomini, and many others, he has contributed to a growing surge of interest in writing poetry in the local dialects, which are linked, for the most part, with Italy's ancient, plurilinguistic, rural civilization. While the main body of Zanzotto's work is highly intellectual and sophisticated, he has written moving tributes in dialect to places, people, and métiers that have vanished, and to which the passage of time and the poignancy of loss caused by mechanization and urbanization have lent an almost magical aura. The current volume focuses on the Zanzotto of this later period, giving emphasis to the dialect experiments, while buttressing them with poems in Italian with which they share affinities. In *Peasants Wake for Fellini's* Casanova *and Other Poems,* Zanzotto explores the link between language and identity, subverts stereotypical attitudes toward dialect, and poeticizes the mystery of human speech itself.

"Today less than ever," the poet observes, "do we know what *dialects* are, in their infinitesimal capillary movements, and what *languages* are, especially those tending toward a panterrestrial diffusion, nor do we know how their destinies intersect." Linguists point out that it is an empirically observable fact that no two individuals have identical speech. Yet we use the term "language," as in the phrase "the Spanish language," for example, as a general abstraction that allows us to characterize the speech patterns of a large group of human beings. The term "dialect" is an abstraction similar to "language" but it generally covers fewer people. The common associations revolving around language and dialect—hierarchical connotations involving "superior" and "inferior," "original" and "derivative"—indicate the close relationship of social and political issues with linguistic and literary matters.

To be sure, a rich, albeit problematic, relationship concerning language, dialect, and literature has been one of the defining characteristics of Italian civilization throughout its long history. During the Renaissance, in the debates concerning the search for a national literary standard, the language of Tuscany, as codified in the masterpieces of Dante, Petrarch, and Boccaccio, emerged as the literary model to be emulated throughout Italy while the other vernaculars, some of which had also been vehicles of written expression, gradually retreated into their local and regional function as primarily spoken means of communication. From this point onward, writing in one of the numerous Italian dialects became a conscious choice: a gesture that also implied a certain polemical distance from Italian. Over the past five hundred years, Italy has developed a vibrant bilingual literary tradition in which writing in the dialects has interacted with, and grown alongside of, the literature in Standard Italian.

In the contemporary dialect verses of *Peasants Wake for Fellini's* Casanova *and Other Poems,* Zanzotto contributes to the dialect tradition of Italian letters, a tradition exemplified by masterworks like the comedies of Ruzante and Carlo Goldoni in Venetian, the sonnets of Giuseppe Gioacchino Belli and Cesare Pascarella in Romanesco; the plays, poetry, and songs of Salvatore Di Giacomo and Eduardo De Filippo in Neapolitan, and the poems of Carlo Porta and Delio Tessa in Milanese. But since this volume includes poems written in Italian, the mixture of dialect and Italian in *Peasants Wake for Fellini's* Casanova *and Other Poems* mirrors not only Zanzotto's experimental forays in recent decades but also points to the bilingualism of the Italian poetic tradition itself. The reader will find a wide sampling of Italian dialect poetry in Hermann W. Haller's remarkable anthology, *The Hidden Italy: A Bilingual Edition of Italian Dialect Poetry* (Wayne State University Press, 1986), which offers literal prose translations in English of some of the best Italian dialect poetry written over the past two centuries together with extensive commentaries.

The flourishing of Italian dialect poetry in the past two decades, a phenomenon known as the "*poesia neodialettale*" (new dialect poetry), coincides with the regression of the dialects and the emergence, for the first time in Italian history, of a truly national spoken idiom. In 1860, for example, at the time of Italian unification, it is estimated that perhaps as few as 2.5 percent of Italians were able to use the so-called "national" language, that is, Tuscan or Standard Italian, for everyday purposes. The other 97.5 percent of the Italian people communicated in the various regional and local dialects. Over a century of Italian political unification, together with internal migration, military conscription, compulsory schooling, and the mass media, has contributed to changing the relationship between Standard

Italian and the dialects. Linguistic surveys now indicate that by the mid-1980s, some 70 percent of Italians had begun to speak Standard Italian at home, many of them together with their regional dialects.

The widespread use of the dialects as a vehicle for contemporary poetry may be related to other phenomena in Italy and throughout the world—a search for "authenticity," for example, as well as a desire to maintain regional and local identities in the face of an unprecedented cultural homogenization, almost planetary in scope. At the same time, it must be emphasized that no single factor unites the numerous Italian poets who choose to write in a dialect. The reader will find a description of the decline of the dialects, of the current situation regarding Italian as a "national" language in the global arena, and much more, in Zanzotto's essay "Observations on the Meaning and the Situation of the Dialects in Italy in the Late Twentieth Century." Although not written explicitly for the English-language reader, it appears in this volume as an introduction to the complex realm of dialect in general and to the contemporary Italian linguistic situation in particular. In these "Observations," Zanzotto also discusses his collaboration with Fellini. While hinting that he had already begun some experiments in dialect many years before, he notes that the visual images of the film *Casanova* elicited a powerful response that took him in a new direction. Moreover, Zanzotto's reflections on dialect as "a first mystery . . . laden with the vertigo of the past," as "coming from a place where no writing exists," and as a guide to "new realities that are pressing to emerge," provide important insights into orality and dialectality at the close of the twentieth century.

"Dialectality," Zanzotto observes, "for centuries had guaranteed a certain comfortable and implicit feeling of cohesion and duration." In fact, linguists estimate that in medieval Europe the circle of acquaintances of a peasant over his or her entire lifespan would not exceed three hundred people. The familiarity among a circumscribed group of people and an appreciation for the strong sense of identity that results from speaking a common idiom comes through clearly in Zanzotto's poetry gathered here, whether in dialect or in Italian. At the same time, it should be emphasized that our poet is no stranger to the deprivation that characterized peasant existence. In the poetry of his early and middle periods, for example, Zanzotto remarked on the decline of the dialects and depicted the suffering of the Italian peasantry. Pasolini, who railed against what he called "the anthropological mutation of the Italian people," observed in his review of *Pasque* that while Zanzotto treated the peasant world, first of all, poetically, in an ironically Virgilian manner, more important, he depicted it as a social world in crisis by touching on emigration, the marginalization of the elderly, and the collapse of agrarian values.

The historian Eric Hobsbawm has described the passing of peasant civilization, not only in Italy but all over the globe, as the major world historical event of the years between 1947 and 1973:

> Historians of the twentieth century in the third millennium will probably see the century's major impact on history as the one made by and in this astonishing period. For the changes in human life it brought about all over the globe were as profound as they were irreversible. Moreover, they are still continuing. The journalists and philosophical essayists who detected "the end of history" in the fall of the Soviet Empire were wrong. A better case can be made for saying that the third quarter of the century marked the end of the seven or eight millennia of human history that began with the invention of agriculture in the stone age, if only because it ended the long era when the overwhelming majority of the human race lived by growing food and herding animals. (*The Age of Extremes* [New York: Pantheon, 1994], pp. 8–9)

Peasants Wake for Fellini's Casanova *and Other Poems,* while paying homage to the literary and linguistic inventiveness of Joyce's *Finnegans Wake,* also marks the passing of the peasant civilization. In the series of dialect poems dedicated to vanishing trades, "Small and Humble Occupations" (inspired by an eighteenth-century book of Venetian woodcuts but illustrated here by the contemporary artist Augusto Murer), and in the hybrid dialect/Italian composition "Going Out to Sew," which includes the sequence of dialect poems "Where Are They?" Zanzotto draws upon his memories of the rural life of his boyhood. In these poems, as well as in dialect verses dedicated to Montale, Pasolini, Charlie Chaplin, and others, Zanzotto evokes the spirits of people dear to him. But these are not the teary-eyed recollections of an aging poet overcome with nostalgia. On the contrary, although he does indeed celebrate a vanishing world and the memory of friends and loved ones who have gone on, he does so in imitation of the Latin tradition of the Manes, the ancestral spirits who become present through evocation. In a similar fashion, in "Venetian Recitative" and in "Peasants Wake," he conjures forth the female deities of his most distant ancestors: the Veneti, an ancient people, highly civilized, who inhabited the fertile land of the northern Adriatic some three thousand years ago and who worshipped a goddess of healing, Rèitia. The drawing of the (fictitious) paleo-Venetic nail, which bears the inscription "To Rèitia Healer and Weaver," begins the opening text written for Fellini's film and closes Zanzotto's long poem in response to that cinematic experience. Symbolizing the earliest possible written evidence of a spoken language whose origins are lost in the mists of prehistory, this nail stands as a fitting emblem of Zanzotto's deep investment in the local landscape and its cultural traditions.

Peasants Wake not only emphasizes the ancient origins of Zanzotto's dialect; it also refers to a popular social rite that disappeared within living memory, the *filò*. In rural areas of the Veneto until the economic "boom" of the late 1950s and early 1960s, peasants would gather in the stables on winter evenings for storytelling and conversation. As depicted in Ermanno Olmi's film *L'albero degli zoccoli* (The Tree of the Wooden Clogs, 1978), which centers on the peasants of the Bergamo region, these gatherings also provided young people an occasion for courtship.

The relationship between land and people, his land and his people, constitutes one of the central elements of Zanzotto's poetry. In the Italian poems that follow, including the "Zauberkraft" section of "Going Out to Sew," which evokes the Cal Santa quarter of the poet's childhood as a cohesive social unit, as well as in such poems as "Nino in the Eighties," "I Would Like to Know," "Docile, Reluctant," and "Silvery Tangles of Your Wanderings," Zanzotto depicts a mysterious, almost magical symbiosis between human beings and the landscape. *Dietro il paesaggio* (Behind the Landscape), after all, was the title of the poet's first volume, published in 1951. It is fitting, therefore, that *Peasants Wake for Fellini's* Casanova *and Other Poems* takes us into, and sometimes beyond, a vanishing human landscape.

Translators' Note John P. Welle and Ruth Feldman

When this project was first discussed with Andrea Zanzotto in the spring of 1987, the poet voiced two concerns. The first involved the place of his dialect poetry within his work as a whole, a problem that he expressed as follows: "presenting *only* a selection of my dialect poems, without a sufficient knowledge of my other poetry, could give an imprecise idea of my work, within which the dialect is very important, but it constitutes one moment of experimentation among many others" (letter to John P. Welle, April 25, 1987). Dialect poetry, of course, has often, and wrongly, been considered a culturally inferior product. Zanzotto, therefore, voices an understandable fear of being known to English readers only or primarily as a dialect poet, while, as he indicates, his dialect compositions need to be seen as one facet of experimentation among many others. The reader will find a representative sampling of Zanzotto's work from his early and middle periods in *Selected Poetry of Andrea Zanzotto,* edited and translated by Ruth Feldman and Brian Swann (Princeton University Press, 1975), which draws from the five books Zanzotto published between 1951 and 1973.

While our chief intention has been to focus on the dialect phase of Zanzotto's experimentalism, we have also provided a selection of the Italian poems of *Idioma,* together with four new poems. We have chosen these poems primarily for their thematic affinities with the dialect texts, although it was Zanzotto himself who called the new poems to our attention and suggested their inclusion. It is our hope that the sample of Italian poems provided here will augment those in dialect and convey a hint, at least, of some of the thematic interests and qualities of Zanzotto's later poetry. The aforesaid selection makes no pretense of representing the complexity, variety, and sheer poetic brilliance of Zanzotto's major achievement, the trilogy, or "pseudo-trilogy," consisting of *Il Galateo in Bosco, Fosfeni,* and *Idioma,* on which his future reputation will no doubt rest.

The second and perhaps more obvious issue raised by the poet in the initial stages of this project concerns the translations themselves. The principal characteristic of Italian dialect poetry, traditional, or what is called "the new dialect poetry," remains its linguistic alterity, that is, its status as "other" vis-à-vis the national literary standard. It is widely believed, not without reason, that dialect poetry in translation, unless rendered into another dialect or subaltern linguistic form, loses its essential character. Here are Zanzotto's own remarks regarding this problem: "In the translations, therefore, if the passage from Italian to English (or into another language) is already uncertain, the passage from dialect into a foreign language becomes almost impossible. The dialect *cannot* be rendered with Standard English. It would be necessary to find some *patois* or slang that nevertheless was rather widely known in the Anglophone area" (letter to John P. Welle, April 25, 1987).

We have chosen not to follow the path suggested by Zanzotto early on. Encouraged by the successful efforts of such translators of Italian dialect poetry as Miller Williams, Hermann W. Haller, John Du Val, Gaetano Cipolla, and others, we are not convinced that the dialect poems by necessity can *only* be rendered in some kind of English *patois* or slang. It is important to note that a recent German translation of Zanzotto's later poetry, *Lichtbrechung* (Verlag Droschl, 1987), which provides a wide sampling from his trilogy, makes use of a German dialect for the Solighese poems and renders the Italian verses into standard German. Without a doubt, those translations—produced by Donatella Capaldi, Ludwig Paulmichl, and Peter Waterhouse—represent the preferred mode for conveying the relationship between the language and the dialect. Unfortunately, contemporary American English does not afford similar possibilities. Whether one settles for Standard English, as we have done, or attempts to move haphazardly toward some version of the demotic, the risk of distorting the sense of the dialect remains equally great. Comforted by the presence of the originals in this multilingual volume, we have sought a diction that is simple and colloquial, yet dignified. Although it isn't possible to reproduce exactly the tone of the dialect, we have tried to capture some of the singsong cadences and lilt. We have also used rhyme and alliteration to echo the music of the dialect.

We want to make it clear that the dialect poems in this volume do not form a homogeneous group. "Venetian Recitative," for example, solicited by Fellini, is written in a pseudo-Venetian dialect that is part imitation of eighteenth-century literary models, part invention. Zanzotto's language—in that text, at least, as his many notes to the poem make clear, and which are reproduced here almost in their entirety—is itself the product, at some level, of the poet's own linguistic inventiveness. "London Lullaby," also solicited by Fellini, constitutes a different kind of linguistic and poetic artifice. Part nursery rhyme, part lullaby, and replete with untranslatable nonsense words, "London Lullaby" truly challenges the limits of translation. Although we trust this text will not be without interest for the reader, we include it here primarily to complete the picture of the poet's contribution to Fellini's *Casanova*. The poems in Solighese dialect, moreover, including "Peasants Wake" and all the dialect poems that follow, are written in a rural vernacular, which Zanzotto employs, in part, to create a deliberately archaic tone. For this reason, we have opted at times for a slightly archaic diction.

Our translation strategy perhaps best corresponds to what George Steiner calls "faithful but autonomous restatement." We have tried to serve as conduits, as attentive as possible to the semantic level of Zanzotto's use of Venetian, the local dialect, and Italian; and we have attempted to produce a literary translation faithful to the original and to its spirit and natural to our own sense of contemporary American English.

Although Zanzotto has never written "concrete" poetry, in

the strict sense of the term, his texts frequently present unique visual arrangements. For this reason, in the translations from *Idioma* we have retained Zanzotto's method of presenting the titles to individual poems. Titles that appear in italic, right of center, such as "*Peoples*," "*Spheres*," "*Horizons*," and "*Where Are They?*," are meant to appear as suggested themes, or hints, whispered softly by a voice off stage. On the other hand, titles appearing in capital letters, such as "I WOULD LIKE TO KNOW," "NINO IN THE EIGHTIES," "GOING OUT TO SEW," and "SMALL AND HUMBLE OCCUPATIONS," should strike the reader with the commanding force of a lapidary inscription.

In an attempt to reflect another of the unique qualities of Zanzotto's work, we have kept the poet's original notes, except in cases where the translation itself rendered the note superfluous, and have even respected their location in the original texts: some are to be found at the bottom of the page, others at the end of the volume. The abbreviation "T.N." stands for "Translators' Note" and signifies instances where we felt commentary was needed. We have tried to keep such interventions to a minimum. The "Orthographic Note" written by Zanzotto refers to all of the dialect poems in this volume.

Acknowledgments

We would like to thank a number of people and institutions for their support. John P. Welle takes this opportunity to thank Gabriel Berns and Johanna Bankier, directors of the Summer Institute on Literary Translation sponsored by the National Endowment for the Humanities held at the University of California, Santa Cruz, in July 1987. The present translations began to take shape between the readings and lively discussions on literary translation held on the wooded campus overlooking Monterey Bay and benefited from the comments of the other participants. It is a pleasure to recall here conversations with Barbara Marti Dooley, a former colleague at the University of Notre Dame, who provided assistance with understanding the nuances of the Venetian and Solighese dialects. Allen Mandelbaum's encouragement of this enterprise has been invaluable. At all times, Andrea Zanzotto himself has been most generous in providing advice about difficult passages.

Some earlier versions of these translations appeared in *Modern Poetry in Translation* (3 [Summer 1993]: 107–14); portions of the introduction, in a different form, have been published in the *Dictionary of Literary Biography,* volume 128, edited by G. De Stasio, G. Cambon, and A. Illiano (Gale Research, 1993), and in *Twentieth-Century Italian Poetry: An Anthology,* edited by John Picchione and Lawrence R. Smith (University of Toronto Press, 1993). The Italian versions of "Venetian Recitative," "London Lullaby," and "Peasants Wake" have been transcribed from the dialect by Tiziano Rizzo. We are grateful to Arnoldo Mondadori Editore, Zanzotto's publisher; to Federico Fellini, whose drawings grace this volume although, sadly, he did not live to see this project completed; to the family of Augusto Murer for the drawings that accompany "Small and Humble Occupations"; and to Angelina Sari, whose drawing of Zanzotto appears on the jacket of this book, and Giorgio Checchin, who facilitated our access to the drawing. We appreciate the assistance of the editorial staff of the University of Illinois Press. We are especially grateful to Veronica Scrol, for her enthusiastic support of this project, and to Carol Bolton Betts, whose dedication, skill, and numerous suggestions contributed immeasureably to the book's improvement. Finally, we wish to thank the Institute for Scholarship in the Liberal Arts, College of Arts and Letters, University of Notre Dame, directed by Jennifer Warlick, for a subvention that made it possible to publish this volume in a multilingual format.

Peasants Wake for Fellini's *Casanova* and Other Poems

From *Filò per il Casanova di Fellini*

(Peasants Wake for Fellini's *Casanova*)

I FOR FELLINI'S *CASANOVA* PER IL CASANOVA DI FELLINI

Rome, July 1976

Dear Andrea,

. . . and now I have to dub it, this film which I have shot recklessly in English, and among the many problems there is also that of the Veneto dialect. In accordance with Naldini's timely suggestion, when I revealed my fears to him, I thought I could write to you for help in finding a key. And I'm writing you now, a bit hesitant, because deep down I don't really know what I want and I hate to bother you. My intention is confused, I have no idea whether my proposal is achievable.

I'll try to convey it to you: I would like to try to break the opacity, the convention of the Veneto dialect which, like all dialects, is frozen in an emotionless and tiresome cipher, and to try to restore freshness to it, render it more alive, penetrating, mercurial, keen, giving preference perhaps to a Ruzantian Veneto dialect or attempting a capricious promiscuity between that of Ruzante and the Veneto dialect of Goldoni. Better yet, rediscovering archaic forms or indeed inventing phonetic and linguistic combinations in such a way that the verbal endeavor also reflects the reverberation of the confused visionariness that I seem to have given to the film.

I admit that these remain only intentions, because, as inevitably happens, the concrete exigencies of the dubbing, the lack of time, the inadequacies of those who have to give voice and expression to these verbal and phonetic inventions, will end up reducing, undramatizing, and rendering only approximate the proposal that I have revealed to you. But isn't it perhaps pleasurable in and of itself to talk fancifully about intentions and ideal realizations even if they prove impractical, in the end?

There is another thing that I would like to ask you: the film begins with a rite (which I have invented) at which the doge, the authorities, and the Venetian people are present. It is a rite enacted at night on the Grand Canal from whose depths a gigantic and black head of a woman must emerge: a kind of lagoon deity, the Great Mediterranean Mother, the mysterious female who lives in each of us. I could go on for a while longer, rashly and imprudently, submitting other suggestive psychoanalytic images.

The ceremony is to some extent the ideological metaphor for the entire film. In fact, at a certain point, the obscure and grandiose fetish—which has not yet completely surfaced—turns to submerge itself because the piles are broken, some of the ropes tear; in short, the great head must return to the depths (sinking in the waters) of the Canal, to remain down there on the bottom forever, unknown and unreachable.

Like every ritual that, in order to become a liberating element, needs to feed on an enkindled psychic force expressed in verbal or mimetic formulas, so too the emergence, the appearance of the dark female simulacrum, should be accompanied by propitiatory prayers, repeated pleas, seductive sounds, evocative litanies and also irreverences, challenges, insults, provocations, grimaces, a gamut of uneasy scepticism to exorcise the dreaded failure of the event. In short, I would like to envelop the whole rite in this fabric, this kind of spider web, sonorous, sacred, and popular. Am I asking too much if I ask you to invent and to write these exhortations, this sad and scoffing prayer, frightened and mischievous, as old as the world and eternally childish?

I'm not through with my questions, dear Andrea, there's still something else I would like to ask you: in London Casanova meets a giantess, originally from the Veneto, who, as a result of an unhappy marriage, has ended up as a sideshow phenomenon in a miserable carnival. The locations, the situations, the atmosphere in which the meeting takes place, the very aspect of this extraordinary female incarnation, make up that mosaic of childish shudders, painful, fabulous, and terrifying, which most emblematically defines Casanova's neurotic relationship with women, i.e., with something obscure, engulfing, overwhelming. At a certain moment, in her tent, the giantess takes a bath in a huge tub together with two Neapolitan dwarf attendants, her only friends, and at the same time she sings a sad, childish little tune. In this instance as well, I imagine a nursery rhyme constructed with the phonetic and linguistic materials of that baby-talk language you rediscovered while you were in Pieve di Soligo. Allow me to quote:

> It's sweet to go elegizing as autumn moves in elegy,
> to collect oneself and thus secretly collect clearings in gold . . .
>
> . . . .
>
> ("Mama e nona te dà ate e cuco e pepi e memela.
> Bono ti, ca, co nona. Béi bumba bona. É fet foa e upi.")[1]

It seems to me that the liquid sonority, the confused gurgling, the sounds, the syllables that melt in the mouth, that sweet broken baby's singsong in a mixture of milk and dissolved solids, a sleep-inducing lapping sound reproposes and suggests efficaciously the kind of subaqueous iconography that characterizes the film, the placental, amniotic image of a decomposed and shifting Venice of algae, mossiness, and musty dank darkness.

That's all, dear Andrea. Of course you should see the film before deciding anything. We'll be able to discuss everything in a somewhat less feverish and more precise way.

This letter doesn't intend in any way to press an immediate assent from you. What I have said to you was rather an attempt to clarify for myself what I have in mind and to entrust it to a poet-friend who by sensitivity and linguistic imagination seems to me the most authoritative and congenial interlocutor for a project dear to my heart . . .

Federico Fellini

1. Translation by Ruth Feldman and Brian Swann, *Selected Poetry of Andrea Zanzotto* (Princeton University Press, 1975), p. 241.

VENETIAN RECITATIVE RECITATIVO VENEZIANO

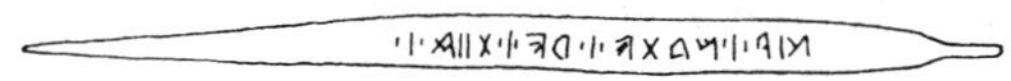

RÈITIAI S'AINÀTEI VEBÈLEI[1]

Vera figura, vera natura,
slansada in ragi come 'n'aurora,
che tutti quanti ti ne inamora:
to fià xe 'l vento, siroco o bora
che svegia sgrìsoli de vita eterna,
signora d'oro che ne governa

aàh Venessia aàh Regina aàh Venùsia

A RÈITIA SANATRICE TESSITRICE

Vera figura, vera natura,
slanciata in raggi come un'aurora,
che tutti quanti ci innamori:
tuo fiato è il vento, scirocco o bora
che desta brividi di vita eterna,
signora d'oro che ci governa

aàh Venezia aàh Regina aàh Venùsia

TO RÈITIA HEALER AND WEAVER

Real figure, real nature,
flung out in rays like the rising sun,
bringing love to life in everyone:
your breath is the wind, sirocco or bora
stirring shivers of life that has no end,
Golden Lady who governs us

ah Venice ah Regina ah Venùsia

1. This is an initial dedicatory shout, of opening. Obviously impossible (given that in the 1700s the paleo-Venetic language was unknown . . .). And Rèitia is the principal (feminine) divinity of the Veneti. *T.N.*: Venetic is an Indo-European language of northeastern Italy, known from inscriptions from the fourth to the second century B.C. The Veneti, an ancient people of northeastern Italy, who preferred commerce and horse breeding to war, aided the Romans against the Gauls and Hannibal. Although the Veneti were absorbed by the Romans after the Second Punic War, they retained local autonomy.

On the poem's title page: the drawing represents a paleo-Venetic nail, highly stylized, with the wording S'AINÀTEI RÈITIAI (in runes that are to be read from right to left). This nail does not exist, but it has been reconstructed by Fabio Z. by mounting the inscription, which had been arranged differently, on the basis of the illustrations to pages 148-49 of *La lingua venetica*, vol. 1, by G. B. Pellegrini and A. L. Prosdocimi, Padua 1967.

DOGE:

Veni amica mea, columba mea,[1]
veni sponsa, veni—
Osculabor labia tua, ubera tua,
ubera tua dulciora vino—

Veni, consurge nobis

(tagliando il nastro)
Resecabo ligamina placentae tuae
ut fulgidior nobis nascaris.

DOGE:

Vieni amica mia, colomba mia,
vieni sposa, vieni—
Bacerò le tue labbra, i tuoi seni,
i tuoi seni più dolci del vino—

Vieni, lèvati fino a noi

Taglierò i legami della tua placenta
perché più fulgida tu nasca a noi.

DOGE:

Come my friend, my dove,
come my bride, come—
I will kiss your lips, your breasts,
your breasts sweeter than wine—

Come, rise up here to us

(he cuts the ribbon)
I will cut the bonds of your placenta
so you will be born to us more dazzling.

1. This is a paraphrase-variation of the *Song of Songs*.

Oci de bissa, de basilissa,[1]
testa de fogo che 'l giasso inpissa,
nu te preghemo: sbrega su fora,
nu te inploremo, tutto te inplora;
móstrite sora, vien su, vien su,
tiremo tuti insieme, ti e nu

aàh Venessia aàh Venissa aàh Venùsia

Occhi di biscia, di regina,
testa di fuoco che accende il ghiaccio,
noi ti preghiamo: erompi su, fuori,
noi t'imploriamo, tutto t'implora;
mostrati sopra, sali, sali,
tiriamo tutti insieme, tu e noi

aàh Venezia aàh Venissa aàh Venùsia

Eyes of a snake, eyes of a queen,
head of fire that inflames the ice,
we beg you: burst loose, break free,
we implore you, everything implores you;
show yourself above, rise up, rise up,
let's all pull together, you and us

ah Venice ah Venissa ah Venùsia

1. *Basilissa*: "regina" (in Greek) with reference to the figures of the mosaics (but also to the mysterious basilisk). *T.N.*: "*Basilissa*" was still circulating in Venetian dialect in the 1970s, indicating a rather bad old woman with a bit of the serpent in her.

Testa santissima, piera e diamante,
boca che parla, rece che sente,
mente che pensa divinamente,
vien su, futuro nostro, vien, dài,
dài baranài tananài tatafài,[1]
sgorlemo i sissi missiemo i sonai[2]

aàh Venessia aàh Vanègia aàh Venùsia

Testa santissima, pietra e diamante,
bocca che parla, orecchi che sentono,
mente che pensa divinamente,
sali, futuro nostro, deh vieni,
dài baranài tananài tatafài,
scuotiamo i sistri rimescoliamo i sonagli

aàh Venezia aàh Vanègia aàh Venùsia

Most holy head, stone and diamond,
mouth that speaks, ears that hear,
mind whose thoughts dwell on high,
rise up, our future, and come near,
come on *baranài tananài tatafài*,
let's shake the sistrums, jiggle the rattles

ah Venice   ah Vanègia   ah Venùsia

1. *Baranài tananài*, etc.: pseudo-Cabalistic jocose words that go back to the tradition of the Zanni. *T.N.*: The Zanni were a type of stock figure, i.e., the poor servant, in the *Commedia dell'arte*, a popular Italian comedy with masked entertainers, which extended across Europe between the sixteenth and the eighteenth centuries.

2. *Sistrums* (an ancient Egyptian percussion instrument) and *rattles* also have a sexual overtone: testicles.

O come ti cressi, o luna dei busi fondi,
o come ti nassi, cavegi blu e biondi,
nu par ti, ti par nu,[1]
la gran marina no te sèra più,
le gran barene[2] de ti se inlaga,
vien su, dragona de arzento, maga!

aàh Venessia   aàh Venaga   aàh Venùsia

O come cresci, o luna dei baratri fondi,
o come nasci, capelli blu e biondi,
noi per te, tu per noi,
il grande mare più non ti rinserra,
le grandi barene di te si allagano,
sali, dragona d'argento, maga!

aàh Venezia   aàh Venaga   aàh Venùsia

Oh how you're growing, oh moon of deep chasms,
oh how you're rising, hair blonde and blue,
you for us, we for you,
the great sea no longer holds you back,
you make a lake from marsh and grass,
rise, silvery dragon, sorceress!

Ah Venice   ah Venaga   ah Venùsia

1. *Nu par ti, ti par nu:* a variation of a well-known expression "*nu co ti, ti co nu,*" signifying the lien existing between Venice and the cities of her territories.

2. *Barene:* sandy and grassy tracts over which the water of the lagoon extends and retreats.

Putina perla, putina unica
che zó ti fifi ne la to cuna,
che zó ti slìmeghi[1] che zó ti bùleghi,
vien ne la rede, fane fortuna,
dane in amor la to manina bela[2]
fata a penèla fata a penèla[3]

aàh Venessia aàh Venùlula aàh Venùsia

Bambina perla, bambina unica
che piagnucoli giù nella culla,
che laggiù stilli che laggiù brulichi,
vieni nella rete, facci fortuna,
dacci in amore la tua manina bella
fatta a penèla fatta a penèla

aàh Venezia aàh Venùlula aàh Venùsia

Pearl of a baby, unique child
who whimpers down in the cradle's depths,
down there you swarm, down there you ooze,
come into the net, bring us good luck,
give us your little hand to touch, to touch,
fashioned so perfectly so perfectly

ah Venice   ah Venùlula   ah Venùsia

1. *Slìmeghi* (ooze): the way a snail moves, leaving a silvery trail behind it.

2. *Give us your little hand:* from a nursery rhyme that is still recited while caressing the hands of little babies.

3. Perhaps "made with the point of a paint-brush," perfectly.

(mentre la testa comincia ad emergere—due voci contrapposte)

(*Vox caelestis*)	(*Vox populi*)	(*Voce celeste*)	(*Voce del popolo*)
—Anadyoméne[1]	—Gira le caéne	Anadyoméne	Gira le catene
—Spuma del mare	—Tira, conpare	Spuma del mare	Tira, compare
—Arca d'alleanza	—Inbraga co creansa	Arca d'alleanza	Imbraca con garbo
—Fulgore amante	—Forsa co le mànteghe!	Fulgore amante	Forza con le manovelle!
—Luce al suo primo vagito	—Fé leva, go dito!	Luce al suo primo vagito	Fate leva, ho detto!
—Seno e sogno dell'alga	—Òcio, che la bala	Seno e sogno dell'alga	Attenti, oscilla

(while the head begins to emerge—two contrasting voices)

(*Celestial Voice*)
—Anadyoméne
—Foam of the Sea
—Ark of the Covenant
—Loving Brightness
—Light at its first cry
—Breast and Dream of Seaweed

(*Voice of the People*)
—Turn the chains
—Pull, my friend
—Harness her gently
—Hurry up with the cranks!
—Jack her up, I said!
—Watch out, she's swaying

1. *Anadyoméne:* Venus Rising from the Waves (accented in the Greek manner).

(mentre cominciano le difficoltà e poi si aggravano)

Signora granda, testa che massa
massa ne passa, che quasi ne schissa,
Dia dei sostegni de cese e palassi
Dia de le taje[1] che su ne tien fissi
Dia de le onde che le ne fa grassi,
ne ingrassa de ogni grassia, Dia Venessia—

aàh Venessia aàh Venàssia aàh Venùsia

Signora grande, testa che troppo
troppo ci sopravanza, che quasi ci schiaccia,
Dea dei sostegni di chiese e palazzi
Dea dei tronchi che ci reggono saldi,
Dea delle onde che ci fanno ricchi,
ci colman di ogni grazia, Dea Venezia—

aàh Venezia aàh Venàssia aàh Venùsia

(while the difficulties begin and then grow worse)

Great lady, head that by far
by far surpasses us, that almost crushes us,
Goddess of the foundations of churches and palaces
Goddess of the piles that support us soundly,
Goddess of the waves that make us rich,
that fill us with every grace, Goddess Venice—

ah Venice   ah Venàssia   ah Venùsia

1. *Taje* (tree trunks) cut to make the piles that support the majority of the buildings in Venice.

Varda parona 'ste strasse, 'sti brassi,
varda tra i ori 'sti povarassi,
buta su l'ocio, móntete su,
tìrene su, nu da ti, ti da nu,
date da far par farne frutar
fruti partuto, par tera e par mar—

aàh Venessia   aàh Frutagna[1]   aàh Venùsia

Guarda padrona questi stracci, queste braccia,
guarda tra gli ori questi poveracci,
alza lo sguardo, levati su,
tirati su, noi da te, tu da noi,
datti da fare per farci fruttare
frutti dovunque, per terra e per mare—

aàh Venezia   aàh Frutagna   aàh Venùsia

Look mistress at these rags, these arms,
see amidst great wealth these wretched souls,
lift up your gaze, stand tall,
stand free, we from you, you from us,
busy yourself and make us fruitful,
fruits everywhere, on land and sea—

ah Venice   ah Frutagna   ah Venùsia

1. *Frutagna*, cf. "Frutana," a proper paleo-Venetic feminine name.

Metéghe i feri, metéghe i pai,
butéghe in gola 'l vin a bocai,
incoconéla de bon e de mègio;
la xe inbriagona, la xe magnona,
ma chissà dopo ma chissà dopo
cossa che la ne dona!—

aàh Venessia   aàh Venàia   aàh Venùsia

Mettetele i ferri, mettetele i pali,
buttatele in gola vino a boccali,
ingozzatela di ogni cosa buona, migliore;
è un'ubriacona, è una mangiona,
ma chissà dopo ma chissà dopo
che cosa ci dona!—

aàh Venezia   aàh Venàia   aàh Venùsia

Put the irons on her, put the stakes to her,
fill her throat with buckets of wine,
cram her full of everything good, everything fine;
she's a glutton, she's a drunkard,
but later who knows, who knows later,
what gifts she'll give us in return!—

ah Venice   ah Venàia   ah Venùsia

Toco de banda, toco de gnòca,[1]
squínsia e barona che a nu ne tóca
par sposa e mare, niora e comare,
sorela e nona, fiola e madona,
ónzete, smòlete, sbrìndola[2] in su—
nu par ti, ti par nu—

aàh Venessia   aàh Venòca   aàh Venùsia

Pezzo di banda, pezzo di gnoca,
civetta e traditrice che a noi càpita
come sposa e madre, nuora e madrina,
sorella e nonna, figlia e suocera,
ungiti, smollati, oscilla in su—
noi per te, tu per noi

aàh Venessia   aàh Venòca   aàh Venùsia

What a dame, what a gal,
flirt and betrayer who's wished on us all,
as bride and mother, daughter-in-law, godmother,
sister and grandma, daughter, and wife's mother,
anoint yourself, loosen, swing yourself high—
we for you, you for us

ah Venice   ah Venòca   ah Venùsia

1. *Banda, gnòca:* "dame" and also "girl."
2. *Sbrìndola:* "swing" (and "turn," "wander").

Ma cossa xelo che zó te striga
ma cossa xelo che zó te intriga;
mona ciavona, cula cagona,
baba catàba,[1] vecia spussona,
nu te ordinemo, in suór e in laór,
che su ti sboci[2] a chi te sa tór—

aàh Venessia   aàh Strùssia   aàh Venùsia

Ma che cos'è che giù ti strega
ma che cos'è che giù ti intrica;
mona chiavona, cula cagona,
baba catàba, vecchia puzzona,
noi ti ordiniamo, in sudore e in lavoro,
che su tu sbocci a chi ti sa prendere—

aàh Venezia   aàh Affanno   aàh Venùsia

What's got you in its spell down there,
what is it that has you all wrapped up;
horny old whore, stinky old slut,
buggy babushka, crazy old bat,
we order you, with sweat and labor
to open yourself to the best taker—

ah Venice   ah Trouble   ah Venùsia

1. *Baba:* "old woman," pejorative (from Slavic); *catàba:* a nonsense word (from the Greek *katabainein,* "to sink"?).
2. *Sbocchi* and *sbocci:* "flow" and "open."

(coro in distanza, che si affievolisce)

Ah, la se inpétola senpre de più,
Ah, la ne casca via da le sate
fora dal piato,
'sta testa maledeta,
'sta redòdesa[1] mata,
la ne sbandona zó inte'l palù,
tuto se scòla, no ghe xe più.

Ah, s'immerda sempre di più,
Ah, ci cade via dalle zampe
fuori del piatto,
questa testa maledetta,
questa strega matta,
ci abbandona giù nella palude,
tutto va a pezzi, non c'è più.

(chorus in the distance, becoming fainter)

Ah, she's getting more screwed up,
Ah, she's losing her footings
off the plate,
this cursed head,
this crazy witch,
she's leaving us down in the bog,
it's all falling apart, gone to the dogs.

1. *Redòdesa*: *befana*, "witch" (from Herodotus?).

(crollo del simulacro, sprofondamento, smarrimento—voci varie)

—Ciò, la crepa —Schrecklisch!
—Odìo, la smama
—Odìo, s'ciòpa soto, tuto quanto
—Malheur, malheur!
—La sbrissa
—La smona
—Se scavessa, se destrude, se désfa —Ça crève
—Dio, cossa nasse —Gefährlich!
—Stòrzela —Ciàpela —Inpìrela
—Segnémose
—Segnémose co la crose
—Ghe gera un crèpo, drento
—Lo gò sentio
—No la vedemo più
—Tasi, tasi, no vogio saver gnente
—'Ndemo via subito
—Jamais vu une chose si morne!
—Voltemo 'l culo, via, via!
—Via, via, desgrassie!
—Mah, no se sa, giremo 'l canton
—Eine Katastrophe!
—Mah mah mah

—Ecco, si sgretola —Terribile!
—Oddìo, sfugge via
—Oddìo, scoppia sotto, tutto quanto
—Disgrazia, disgrazia!
—Scivola
—Non se ne può più
—Si spezza, si distrugge, si sfa —Schiatta
—Dio, che cosa accade —Pericoloso!
—Torcila —Prendila —Infilzala
—Segniamoci
—Segniamoci con la croce
—C'era una fenditura, dentro
—L'ho percepita
—Non la si vede più
—Taci, taci, non voglio saper niente
—Andiamo via subito
—Mai veduta una cosa sì tetra!
—Via, frégatene, via, via!
—Via, via, disgrazie!
—Mah, non si sa, tagliamo l'angolo.
—Una catastrofe!
—Mah mah mah

(collapse of the image, sinking, bewilderment—various voices)

—Look, she's crumbling —How awful!
—Oh God, she's slipping away
—Oh my God, the whole thing's exploding down below
—Disaster! Disaster!
—She's sliding
—She can't take it any more
—She's breaking, falling apart, dissolving —She's bursting
—God, what's going on —This is dangerous!
—Twist her —Grab her —Tie her together
—Let's cross ourselves
—Let's make the sign of the cross
—There was a crack, inside
—I'd noticed it
—We can't see her anymore
—Shut up, shut up, I don't want to know about it
—Let's get out of here right now
—I've never seen anything so ghastly!
—Get out of here, screw it, go! go!
—Go! Get going! A misfortune!
—My God! I don't know, let's cut across the corner.
—A catastrophe!
—I can't believe it!

—Me vien un travaso de sangue
—Dunkles Schicksal!
—Mah   mah   mah
—Malora

—Mi viene un trasalimento, un soprassalto
—Destino oscuro!
—Mah   mah   mah
—Malora

—I'm really startled, what a blow!
—Dark fate!
—I don't know, I just don't know
—Ruin! It's ruin!

LONDON LULLABY CANTILENA LONDINESE

Pin penin[1]
valentin
pena bianca
mi quaranta
mi un mi dói mi trèi mi quatro
mi sinque mi sie mi sète mi òto
buròto
stradèa
comodèa—

Pin penin[2]
fureghin
perle e filo par inpirar[3]
e pètena par petenar
e po' codini e nastrini e cordèa—

le xe le comedie i zoghessi de chéa
che jeri la jera putèa[4]

Piè-piedino
valentino
penna bianca
io quaranta
io uno io due io tre io quattro
io cinque io sei io sette io otto
buròto
stradèa
comodèa—

Piè-piedino
ficchino
perle e filo per infilzare
e pettine per pettinare
e poi codini e nastrini e cordicella—

sono i giocuzzi i giochini di quella
che ieri era bambina.

Pin penin
valentin
Old Mother Goose when she wanted to wander
would ride through the air on a very fine gander.
One, two, buckle my shoe,
three, four, close the door,
five, six, pick up sticks,
seven, eight, lay them straight,
nine, ten, a big fat hen—

Pin penin
fureghin
pearls and thread for stringing,
little combs for preening,
pigtails, hair-ribbons and fine cord—

these are the games, the foolish play,
of the girl who was a child only yesterday.

1. This is an ancient and very widespread ditty, a bit modified (and one moreover that has many local variants) with numerous untranslatable nonsense words. The language presents very wide fluctuations within the (or "a") *koiné* of the Veneto, which is as much spatial as temporal.

2. The invented part begins here. *T.N.*: After emulating the spirit of the original in the opening stanza, the translation begins to render the literal meaning as closely as possible while retaining the initial nonsense words of each stanza.

3. An allusion to the Venetian craft of the *inpiraresse*, unparalleled craftswomen, stringers of tiny pearls used in the most delicate artistic works.

4. In the original, the distortions into baby-talk become heightened.

Pin pidin
cossa gastu visto?
'Sta piavoleta nua
'sto corpesin 'ste rosete
'sta viola che te consola
'sta pele lissa come séa
'sti pissigheti de rissi
'sti oceti che te varda fissi
e che sa dir "te vói ben"
'ste suchete 'sta sfeseta—

le xe le belesse da portar a nosse
a nosse conposte[1] de chéa
che jeri la jera putèa

Piè-piedino
che hai visto?
Questa bambolina nuda
questo corpicino queste rosette
questa viola che ti consola
questa pelle liscia come seta
questi riccioli pizzichini
questi occhietti che ti guardano fissi
e che san dire "ti voglio bene"
queste zucchette questa fessurina—

sono le bellezze da portare a nozze
nozze composte di quella
che ieri era bambina.

Pin pidin
what have you seen?
This naked little doll,
this body so small, these rosettes,
this violet to take comfort in,
this silk-smooth skin,
these tiny curls that tickle,
eyes that watch you intently too,
and seem to be saying "I love you,"
these little pumpkins, this tiny slit—

these are the fine things fit for a wedding,
a glorious wedding for the little girl,
who yesterday was a child at play.

1. "A glorious wedding": like those at the end of fairy tales.

Pin penin
valentin
o mio ben,
te serco inte'l fogo inte'l giasso[1]
te serco e no ghe riesso
te serco e no ghe la fasso,
pan e dedin
polenta e nasin—
chi me fa dormir
chi me fa morir
tuta pa'l me amor
chi me fa tornar
coi baseti che ciùcia
coi brasseti che struca
co la camiseta più bèa—

le xe le voje i caprissi de chéa
che jeri la jera putèa

Piè-piedino
valentino
o mio bene,
ti cerco nel fuoco nel ghiaccio
ti cerco e non ci riesco
ti cerco e non ce la faccio,
pane e ditino
polenta e nasino—
chi mi fa dormire
chi mi fa morire
tutta per il mio amore
chi mi fa tornare
coi bacetti che succhiano
con le braccine che stringono
con la camicetta più bella—

sono le voglie i capricci di quella
che ieri era bambina

Pin penin
valentin
oh, my dear,
I search for you in ice and fire,
I search but never find you,
I search and search and can't go on,
bread and tiny toes
polenta and tiny nose—
who makes me sleep,
who makes me die,
all for my love
who makes me return
with lingering kisses
with close embraces
with the prettiest blouse—

these are the wishes, the whims of the girl,
who yesterday was a child at play.

1. Here begins the almost obligatory theme of the futile search, a theme relevant for the entire film.

Pin pidin
valentin
pan e vin
o mio ben,
un giosso, solo che un giosso,
te serco drento inte'l masso
te serco fora dal masso
te serco te serco e indrío sbrisso,
chi xe che me porta 'l mio ben
chi me descanta
chi me desgàtia
chi me despìra,
pan e pidin
polenta e nasin
polenta e late
da le tetine mate
   da le tetine beate—

i xe i zoghessi de la piavoleta
le xe le nosse i caprissi de chéa
de chéa
che jeri la jera putèa.

Piè-piedino
valentino
pane e vino
o mio bene,
un goccio, soltanto un goccio,
ti cerco dentro il mazzo
ti cerco fuori del mazzo
ti cerco ti cerco e scivolo indietro,
chi mi porta il mio bene
chi mi disincanta
chi mi sgroviglia
chi mi sfilza,
pane e piedino
polenta e nasino
polenta e latte
dalle tettine matte
   dalle tettine beate—

sono i giocuzzi della bambolina
sono le nozze i capricci di quella
di quella
che ieri era bambina.

Pin penin
valentin
bread and wine,
oh my sweet,
a drop, a little dribble,
I search for you in the bouquet,
I search for you outside it too,
I search and search, then slip behind,
who will bring my love to me,
who will end the magic spell,
who'll set me free,
who will unstring me,
bread and tiny toes
polenta and little nose
polenta and milk
from the crazy little breasts
   from the happy little breasts—

this is the make-believe of the little doll,
the wedding and the whims of the girl,
of the girl
who yesterday was a child at play.

II PEASANTS WAKE FILÒ

PEASANTS WAKE FILÒ

No dighe gnént del cine[1]—
vorìe parlar del cine—
al me strassina 'l cine—
me fa spavento 'l cine—
parché 'l zharvèl al ne inpignis de bòcoi
de color velenà squasi senpre,
parché 'l ne slózha spes
i pra e i bòsch de le nostre àneme debole
—là sote e dentro, dó inte 'l bas—
co la plastica del só celuloide[2]
che gnént l'é bon de inciucar-dó, gnént de paidir.
E ò squasi maledì
tante òlte 'sti posti de cine
che cofà bue sbusa fin fora pa' i camp,
no pi sol che in paesi e zhità:
a inpastrociarne i nostri insònii

Non dico niente del cinema—
vorrei parlare del cinema—
mi trascina via il cinema—
mi fa spavento il cinema—
perché il cervello ci riempie di bolle e boccioli
di colore avvelenato quasi sempre,
perché spesso ci lorda
i prati e i boschi delle nostre anime deboli
—là sotto e dentro, giù dentro il profondo—
con la plastica della sua celluloide
che niente è capace di inghiottire, né digerire.
E ho quasi maledetto
tante volte questi luoghi di cinema
che come piaghe bucano perfino in piena campagna,
non più soltanto in paesi e città:
a impiastricciare i nostri sogni

I'm not talking about movies—
I'd like to talk about movies—
I get carried away by movies—
I'm scared by movies—
because they fill our brains with bubbles and buds
almost always a poisonous color,
lots of times they soil for us
the meadows and woods of our weak souls
—there, under and inside, way down in the depths—
with the plastic of their celluloid
that can't swallow or digest anything.
And plenty of times I've almost cursed
these movie places
that riddle the countryside like sores,
no longer just in towns and cities:
to muck up our dreams

1. This is also true in analogous/different ways for television . . .

2. *Celluloid*: a term used mostly in honor of a tradition. Films and "plastic" of various types are always related in some way to artificial polymers, everpresent. Moreover, they are very useful.

On the title page: Filò: the evening gathering of peasants in the stables during the winter, but also an endless conversation that serves to pass the time and nothing else.

e 'l parlar dei insònii
che tutte le maniere de crearse e inventarse
al sèra in lu: ne ciùcia, 'l cine, 'l ne fa a tòch,
co la so fórfese 'l ne strazha, 'l ne reinpéta,
inte le so moviole 'l ne straòlta,
al ghe roba 'l so propio DNA[1]
al grop che é pi scondést de noaltri stessi
dó inte 'l pos senzha fondi.
Ma qualche òlta 'l cine arzh brusa e fa ciaro
come si 'l vegnèsse da un incalmo
dei bar de roe de l'Horeb,[2]
al mostra de esser fià broènt de dèi si pur bastardo,
al ne fa s'ciopar sbociar fora come i but a la vèrta
al ne met par trói stranbi, sote zhiéi del tut nóvi,
a calcossa che é là che l' ne spèta, inte 'n gòder,
na siorìa, 'n teren, un vent che no à confin,
e 'l cine—squasi—'l par lu la poesia,
al ciapa-dentro tut in poesia—n'altra.
Ma ben i é rari quei che pól far 'sto cine:
éi spiriti, onbre, barlumère de cine

e il parlare dei sogni
che tutte le maniere di crearci e inventarci
racchiude in sé: ci succhia, il cine, ci fa a pezzi,
con la sua forbice ci straccia, ci riappiccica,
dentro le sue moviole ci stravolge,
ruba il suo proprio DNA
al grumo più nascosto di noi stessi
giù nel pozzo senza fondo.
Ma qualche volta il cinema arde brucia e illumina
come se venisse da un innesto
dei cespugli di rovi dell'Horeb,
mostra di essere fiato bruciante di dèi seppur bastardo,
ci fa scoppiare sbocciar fuori come germogli a primavera
ci immette in sentieri strani, sotto cieli del tutto nuovi,
in qualcosa che è là che ci aspetta, in una gioia
una ricchezza, un terreno, un vento che non ha confini,
e il cinema—quasi—sembra lui la poesia,
cattura tutto in poesia—un'altra.
Ma rari invero son quelli che possono fare questo cinema:
sono spettri ombre allucinazioni di cinema

and the talking about dreams
that contains in itself all the ways we create and invent ourselves:
they suck us in, the movies, tear us apart,
with their scissors they rip us to pieces, patch us together again,
inside their moviolas they knock us out,
they steal their DNA
from the most secret clot of who we are,
down in the well that's got no bottom.
But sometimes movies blaze burn and give light,
as if they sprang from a graft
of Mt. Horeb's bramble bushes,
they show that they're really the flaming breath of gods, however bastard,
they make us burst open and bloom like buds in springtime,
they put us on strange paths, under skies never seen before,
in something that's there waiting for us, a joy,
a richness, some land, a limitless wind,
and movies—they seem almost to be poetry,
they capture everything in poetry—an other.
But they're truly hard to come by, the ones who can make those movies:
are they ghosts, shadows, movie-hallucinations

1. An almost genetic inheritance (like the one that is "closed" in DNA).
2. Horeb: the mount of the burning bush of the biblical God.

nassésti su dal cine lori stessi—pitost che òmi?
Da l'aldelà che l'é 'l cine vegnésti,
póre aldelà, gran aldelà de ciaro e plastica?

• • •

Cussì,[1] co Federico me à mostrà carnevai e Venezhie
che déa s'ciantis e baléa 'fa ale e pavéi
de mili segnati[2] e color
mai strachi de dugar a far fola e missiarse
senzha che se savèsse quel che devero i fusse
né che man né che ocio li 'vèsse buridi fora—;
e co ò vist la gran testa
testa de tut quel che noaltri són,
tirada su desmat e desbòn
tirada su e po' dopo cascar dó
tra sacrabòlti sbìgola e fifìo—
'sta testa che é la nostra salvazhion
e perdizhion, prima, regina, et quidvis amplius

nati su dal cinema essi stessi—anziché uomini?
Da quell'aldilà che è il cinema venuti,
povero aldilà, grande aldilà di luce e plastica?

• • •

Così, quando Federico mi ha mostrato carnevali e Venezie
che davano lampi e ballavano come ali di farfalle
di mille razze e colori
mai stanchi di giocare a far folla e mescolarsi
senza che si sapesse quel che davvero fossero
né che mano né che occhio li avesse scovati fuori—;
e quando ho visto la grande testa
testa di tutto quello che noi siamo,
sollevata per scherzo e sul serio
sollevata e dopo cascar giù
tra imprecazioni, panico, spavento—
questa testa che è la nostra salvezza
e perdizione, primigenia, regina, e qualunque cosa di più grande

born and raised themselves from movies—rather than men?
Have they come from that great beyond called "the movies,"
that poor great beyond of light and plastic?

• • •

And so, when Federico showed me Carnivals and Venices
throwing off flashes and dancing like butterfly wings
of a thousand breeds and colors
never tired of playing swarming
and mixing so nobody could tell what they really were,
or what hand what eye had roused them out—;
and when I saw the great head
head of all that we are,
raised up as a joke and seriously too,
raised up and then falling down
among oaths, shrieks, panic—
this head that is our salvation
and perdition, the source, the queen, *et quidvis amplius*

1. This is the description of the first scene of the film. References to other scenes follow.

2. *Segnati* (breeds) is a learned expression (it comes from the *Book of the Apocalypse*) that has remained in the popular language.

omnibus[1]—; co ò vist tornar 'sta testa
inte quela de un femenon fenomeno da careton
(ma che 'varíe volést esser tatina)
e po' sparir inte i calivi de un'ipnoLondra;
e po' ancora inte 'l jazh
de 'na Venezhia-Caina[2] far bau/sète[3]
(Ah Casanova gramazh, quant che tu 'véa
sol che par éla strussià, strolegà,
e da 'na sfesa a 'n'altra girà 'fa 'n burlo)—
do tre, do tre parole par 'sta dia
me se à movést e slavinà fora, inte 'n parlar
che no l'é qua né là, venizhian sì e no,
lontan vizhin sì e no, ma ligà al me parlar
vecio, de l'ort che bef dal Suligo e dal Gerda,
ligà da radis úgnole.[4]

per tutti—; quando ho visto tornare tal testa
in quella di un donnone fenomeno da circo
(ma che avrebbe voluto essere bambinetta)
e poi sparire nelle nebbie di un'ipnoLondra;
e ancora poi nel ghiaccio
di una Venezia-Caina riaffacciarsi
(ah Casanova poveraccio, quanto avevi
soltanto per lei faticato, almanaccato,
e da una "donna" a un'altra girato come una trottola)—
due tre, due tre parole per questa dea
mi si son mosse, franate fuori, di un parlare
che non è né qua né là, veneziano sì e no,
lontano vicino sì e no, ma legato al mio parlare
vecchio, dell'orto che beve dal Soligo e dal Lierza,
legato da radici uniche.

omnibus—; when I saw this head turn
into that of a circus fat lady
(who would have liked to be a little girl)
and then vanish in the fogs of a hypnoLondon;
and show up again afterwards in the ice
of a Venice-Caina playing peek-a-boo
(Ah poor Casanova, how much you labored
for her alone, building castles in the air,
and from one twat to another you spun like a top)—
two three, two or three words for this goddess
came landsliding out of me, in a dialect
that's neither here nor there, kind of Venetian, yes and no,
far away close at hand, yes/no, but tied to my ancient
tongue, from the orchard that drinks from the Soligo and the Lierza,
bound by single roots.

1. *T.N.*: "and something greater over and beyond everything."

2. *T.N.*: Caina is the outermost circle of the lowest region of Dante's Hell.

3. A game that is played with children. Fort/da . . . *T.N.*: Freud discusses the significance of children's games involving disappearance and return in "Beyond the Pleasure Principle."

4. Roots that are single not double. This refers to the valley of the Soligo and its tributary, the Lierza, almost as small as a backyard garden. But one should also name the Perón, the Campéa, the Follina, the Marzolle, and all the streams, each with their own little valley, that flow into the Soligo and then into the Piave.

Dia, tu me sé tornada-in-qua
da l'aldelà de ciaro mort e morta celuloide:
mal tu me à fat, mal tu me à fat
in laguna in calivo e dentro al jazh,
ma de volerte no ò podést far de manco.
E cussì ò scrit, no so né ché, né cón, né cossa,[1]
e de là me son ris'cià, picolà in fora,
fin a cavar su da chissà onde
fin a sforzharme co 'sta secia sbusada
co 'sto tamiso de maja ramai massa larga
a cavar su 'l parlar vecio, 'sto qua che sentì ades,
quel che par mi l'é de la testa-tera,
creda acqua piera léda
dréta intiera tajada intorcolada
mai vista ben mai tocada co man né rebaltada,
tera che se móf da sote tera
e che scriver me à fat senpre paura
anca si l'ò parlà-parlada
da senpre, dala matina a la sera al sòn de not.

• • •

Dea, mi sei rinvenuta
dall'aldilà di luce morta e morta celluloide:
male mi hai fatto, male mi hai fatto
in laguna in nebbia e dentro il ghiaccio,
ma di volerti non ho potuto fare a meno.
Così ho scritto, non so né che, né come, né cosa,
e di là ho arrischiato, mi sono spenzolato fuori,
fino a cavar su da chissà dove
fino a sforzarmi con questo secchio bucato
con questo setaccio dalla maglia ormai troppo larga
a cavar su il dialetto vecchio, questo che sentite adesso,
quello che per me è della testa-terra,
creta acqua pietra limo
dritta intera tagliata contorta
mai veduta bene mai toccata con mano né rovesciata,
terra che si muove da sotterra
e che scrivere mi ha fatto sempre paura
anche se l'ho parlato-parlata
da sempre, dalla mattina alla sera al sonno notturno.

• • •

Goddess, you came back to me
from the great beyond of dead light and dead celluloid:
you hurt me, you hurt me
in the lagoon in the fog and in the ice,
but I couldn't help wanting you.
And so, I started to write, I don't know what or how,
from there I set out to seek my fortune, I leaned way out,
far enough to bring up from who knows where
far enough to force myself with this leaky pail
this sieve with the now too-wide meshes
to dredge up the old dialect, this one that you're hearing now,
that for me belongs to the earth-Mother,
clay water stone lime
straight whole cut twisted
never seen clearly never touched by hand never overturned,
earth that moves under the earth
a tongue I've always been afraid to write
even if I have spoken it/her
always, from morning to evening to sleep at night.

• • •

1. This last clause is a paraphrase of the interrogative expressions in fairytales, children's songs, and nursery rhymes.

Inte 'sti dì che 'l fret scurta e la ppióva
sòfega—sepulì setenbre[1]
e un an, prima del tenp—,
inte 'ste not che 'l vent ciama e fa fora
co sión de acqua e lanpidar,
fumane e fumeghère—
inverno e istà missiadi cofà cavèi de strighe—,
inte 'ste ore che 'l sol par un momento
libera, e po 'l le mola
a morir inte 'l mój, tra restèi
negri drio i crép de le montagne—
e tut quel che se vet par trat inte 'na cort
anca siben che de ori l'é piena 'sta cort—
santa tera, tu trema. Tera coss'atu, tera?
Anca altre òlte, inte 'l passà, sentìe
'sti sbrissar de colpo, ma picinini, cèi,
'ste pachete lidiére, 'sto buligar scondést.
E quel móverte un póch
cofà bestiola stufa de cavezha
cofà 'na tata in cuna
cofà l'ingrespadura de 'na gran sigurezha e pazhe senzha fin

In questi giorni che il freddo accorcia e la pioggia
soffoca—seppellito settembre
e un anno, prima del tempo—,
in queste notti che il vento chiama e divora
con grandi scrosci d'acqua e lampeggiare,
vampe e fumigamenti—
inverno e estate mischiati come capelli di streghe—,
in queste ore che il sole per un momento
libera, e poi le lascia andare
a morire nel madido, tra cancelli
neri dietro i greppi delle montagne—
e tutto quello che si vede sembra buttato in un letamaio
anche se di ori è pieno il letamaio—
santa terra, tu tremi. Terra, che hai, terra?
Anche altre volte, per il passato, sentivo
questi scivolii improvvisi, ma piccoli, piccolissimi,
questi colpetti leggeri, questo brulicare nascosto.
E quel muoverti un poco
come vaccherella stanca di cavezza
come bambinetta in culla
come l'incresparsi di una sicurezza e pace senza fine

In these days that the cold shortens and the rain
smothers—buried September
and a year before the time—,
in these nights that the wind calls and devours
with torrents of water and lightning,
flashes and smoky globes of mist—
winter and summer tangled like witches' hair—,
in these hours the sun frees for a moment
and then lets go
to die in the wet, between the black
gates behind the mountain rocks—
and everything you see looks as though it's been thrown on a dunghill,
even if the dunghill's full of gold—
holy earth, you're shaking. What's the matter with you, earth?
Other times, too, in the past, I've felt
these sudden slidings, but they were small, tiny,
these light blows, this hidden swarming.
And that slight moving of yours
like a heifer tired of the halter
like a baby girl in a cradle
like the rippling of an endless certainty and peace

1. A reference to the second heavy earthquake of Friuli in 1976, the one in September.

me diséa sol che tu era viva e springa
e cussì tu me déa debòto un gòder—
un s'ciantín spasemà,
insurì ma zentil
'fa un most o un vinel nostro e tóo:
gòder de ti sorela pi che mare,
de ti caoreta fedeta soreleta
persa e despersa in fior e alberi
in gobe e bus de montagnole, in penacét de verdo
e fii de ràin inbarlumidi,
par trói, par rui, par tache
qua e là de neve—dai let de pra a le grémene,
da la bassa a la alta, sote 'l sol.
E si in passà ogni tant, ma tant, tu te sgorléa
de pi (levarse-su de not, ciamarse de faméje,
vache e bò che muléa, can che bajéa)
squasi mai no tu 'véa sassinà,
tu paréa 'ndata in oca, mèda ciòca, senzha pecà mortal.
Ma ancó no l'é cussì. Chi sétu ti? Chi?
Na fedeltà granda la se a sfantà.

• • •

mi diceva soltanto che eri viva e piena di brio
e così tu mi davi quasi un gaudio—
un po' allarmato,
irritato ma gentile
come un mosto o un vinello nostro e tuo:
godere di te sorella più che madre,
di te capretta pecorella sorellina
persa e dispersa in fiori e alberi
in dossi e anfratti di colline, pennacchietti di verde
e ragnateli abbagliati,
per sentieri, per rivi, per chiazze
qua e là di neve—dai letti di prato alle grémene,
dalla piana alle alture, sotto il sole.
E se nel passato ogni tanto, ma tanto, ti scrollavi
di più (alzarsi di notte, chiamarsi di famiglie,
vacche e buoi che mugghiavano, cani che abbaiavano)
quasi mai avevi assassinato,
sembravi caduta in distrazione, mezza ubriaca, senza peccato mortale
Ma oggi non è così. Chi sei tu? Chi?
Una fedeltà grande si è dissolta.

• • •

told me only that you were alive and full of fire
and so you gave me almost a joy—
kind of alarmed,
irritated but pleasant
like must or a young wine, ours and yours:
enjoy yourself, sister more than mother,
little nanny-goat, lambkin, kid-sister,
lost and scattered in flowers and trees
in the heights and gorges of the hills,
in tiny plumes of green and sun-dazzled cobwebs,
over trails and pools, over patches, here and there,
of snow—from the beds of the meadows to the sterile places,
from the plain to the heights, under the sun.
And if in the past ever so often, but often, you shook
harder (getting up in the night, the families calling out,
cattle and oxen bellowing, dogs barking)
you almost never killed anybody,
you seemed distracted, half-drunk, free of mortal sin.
But today's different. Who are you? Who?
A great loyalty has ended.

• • •

Ades, anca di 'sto canton l'é sparagnà
e si qua riva i sèst del tó matìo
senzha far dan—del to matìo bónbo e turbido
in sacra frève e ustinazhion,
del tó saltar e pénder inpresonadi—
no se pól pi cocolarte né pi volerte ben;
ne vien l'ingóssa al cór par i fradei
qua darente, cari fradei furlani,
'pena par là drio 'l vel
che vien su da la piana, drio 'l giro del Canséjo;[1]
e se à paura de 'ste montagne blu
che tant soméja a quele del Furlàn;
se sa che quel che qua ne sgórla e basta
póch lontan schinzha copa désfa tra-dó;
se sa che tu sé furia,[2] pèdo che miér e miér de furie,
salvàrega tremenda irata sphynx
che no se pól vardar sul muso mostro
che non se pól pensar: mare-mostro tu torna
a esser, come senpre, inte 'l momento che
la verità la sfondra, dia che massa

Adesso, anche se quest'angolo è risparmiato
e se qui arriva il gesticolare della tua follia
senza far danno—della tua follia satura e torbida
in sacra febbre e ostinazione,
del tuo saltare e spingere, imprigionati—
non ti si può più coccolare né voler bene;
ci assale uno spasimo per i fratelli
qui vicini, cari fratelli friulani,
appena dietro il velo
che viene su dalla pianura, dietro il giro del Cansiglio;
e si ha paura di questi monti blu
che tanto somigliano a quelli del Friuli;
si sa che ciò che qua ci scuote soltanto
poco lontano schiaccia ammazza sfa demolisce;
si sa che tu sei furia, peggio che migliaia e migliaia di furie,
selvatica tremenda irata sfinge
che non si può guardar sul muso mostro,
che non si può pensare: madre-mostro tu torni
a essere, come sempre, nel momento che
la verità sfonda, dea che troppo

Now, even though this corner has been spared
and the strange gestures of your madness
reach here without doing damage—imprisoned by your gloomy and glutted madness
by your holy fever and stubbornness,
by your leaping and pushing—
we can't snuggle up to you, we can't love you any more;
we're pierced by a sharp pain for our brothers
close by, dear brothers of Friuli,
only just behind the veil
rising up from the plain, behind the circle of the Cansiglio;
and we're afraid of these blue mountains
that look a lot like those in Friuli;
we know that what in these parts hardly shakes,
not far away crushes kills rips down demolishes;
we know you to be a fury, worse than thousands and thousands of furies
terrible enraged savage sphinx
we can't look at your angry pock-marked face
we can't imagine you: you go back to being,
mother/monster, as always, in the moment
truth breaks through, goddess,

1. Peaks, high plain, and forest of the Cansiglio.

2. *Furia* ("fury") also has the meaning, more common, of "haste," which is included here.

massa ne passa, o pur
che—cussita 'l dis al libro de la Ginestra[1]—
no tu sa gnént
né de ti né de noi, e 'l tó star l'é come 'l tó sgorlarte
e 'l tó 'ndar par i miér de miér de ani
l'é come un star. Verda tu sé, par senpre,
anca co tu sé sas galivo e stèrp,
tu fioris anca intant che tu copa; inpetrida, tu bój.

Ma fursi l'é che no te són stati drio
che no te 'ón volést bastanzha ben
che no te 'vón studià[2] vena par vena
strica de forzha par strica de forzha,
no te 'ón scoltà da vizhin, co umiltà,
co amor, par quel che tu era:
una—siguro—che póch la ne bada,
ma che de pi l'à fat pa'l nostro ben—senzha volerlo
senzha saverlo—che par al nostro mal

troppo ci sopravanza; oppure
che—così dice il libro della Ginestra—
non sai niente
né di te né di noi, e il tuo stare è come il tuo scrollarti
e il tuo andare per le migliaia di millenni
è come uno stare. Verde sei, per sempre,
anche quando sei sasso liscio e sterile,
fiorisci anche mentre uccidi; coagulata, ribolli.

Ma forse, forse non ti abbiamo corteggiata
non ti abbiamo voluto bene abbastanza
non ti abbiamo studiata vena per vena
linea di forza per linea di forza
non ti abbiamo ascoltato da vicino, umilmente,
con amore, per quello che tu eri:
una—certo—che poco di noi cura
ma che più ha fatto per il nostro bene—senza volerlo
senza saperlo—che per il nostro male,

way way ahead of us, and yet,
—according to the book of the Ginestra—
you know nothing
of yourself or of us, and your stillness is like your trembling,
and your passing through thousands of millennia
is like standing still. You are green, forever,
even when you're a stone smooth and sterile,
you come to life even while you kill; clotted, you start boiling again.

But maybe, maybe we haven't courted you enough
we haven't loved you enough
we haven't studied you vein by vein
force-line by force-line,
we haven't listened to you close up, with humility,
with love, for what you were:
someone—certainly—who cares little for us
but who has done more to help us—without wanting to
or even knowing—than to harm us,

1. *T.N.*: "the book of the Ginestra" refers to the *Canti* of Giacomo Leopardi, and particularly to the poem "La ginestra" (The Broom Plant), which enjoins human beings to band together in a common struggle against nature.

2. *Studiar* ("studied") assumes here also the value of "to make haste with preoccupation about something," in the somewhat more archaic meaning.

(si se pól mai vardar, stralòci, inte 'l stralòcio).
L'à rason quel senpre de la Ginestra:
són stati massa qua a sticar tra òmi
a cavarse i oci un co l'altro
a darse fógo inte le bubarate
infami de le guere e de le inquisizhion
a sbudelarse par tre o quatro pèrteghe
o concòi de pi o in manco,
invezhe che catarse, volerse tuti insieme,
insenbradi a conbater—co amor—contra de ti
mare da maledir e da adorar
che non, nisi parendo, vincitur.[1]
E cossa te 'óne fat, quant te 'óne fat
de mal—intossegada, scassada, rosegada,
castrada—nò pa'l ben nostro che dal tóo no pól partirse,
ma par sganga[2] de póchi, zhus col gòs pien de roba,
stanfadi, inmatonidi,
e pur drio senpre a sgramolar,
par le bave de schèi slacàin marzhi patòchi,
e par chi che dovendo depararne, depararte da lori,

(se, strabici, possiamo mai guardare nello strabismo).
Ha ragione ancora quello della Ginestra:
ci siamo troppo perduti a litigare tra uomini
a cavarci gli occhi l'un l'altro
a incendiarci nei falò
infami delle guerre e delle inquisizioni
a sbudellarci per tre o quattro pertiche
o solchi in più o in meno,
anziché ritrovarci, volerci tutti insieme,
amalgamati a combattere—con amore—contro di te
madre da maledire e da adorare
che è vinta soltanto (alle sue leggi) obbedendo.
E che cosa ti abbiamo fatto, quanto ti abbiamo fatto
di male—intossicata, sconquassata, rosicchiata
castrata—non per il bene nostro che dal tuo non può separarsi,
ma per l'avidità di pochi, gufi dal gozzo pieno
zeppi fino all'intontimento,
e pur sempre intenti a sgranocchiare,
per le bave di soldi lumacosi, marci fradici,
e per colpa di chi dovendo difenderci, e difenderti da loro,

(if, cross-eyed as we are, we can ever look into what is cross-eyed).
He's right again, the man who wrote the *Ginestra*:
we've lost ourselves fighting with other men
ripping out each other's eyes
burning people alive
becoming vile through wars and inquisitions
gutting people for three or four more rods
or furrows
instead of meeting, banding together,
combining forces to fight—with love—against you
mother to damn and to adore
who can be defeated only "If one obeys her laws."
And what we have done to you, how much we have hurt you—
poisoned, smashed, chewed up,
castrated—not for our common good, that can't be separated from yours,
but because of the greed of a few people, rapacious owls with overfull crops,
crammed until stupefied,
and still intent on crunching away,
because of money's snail slime, decaying, rotten,
and because those who were supposed to defend us,

1. *Nisi parendo, vincitur*: "If one obeys her laws." The quotation is from Francis Bacon.
2. *Sganga* ("greed") has the collective meaning of "avidity, eagerness, haste."

ghe tegnéa terzho invezhe.
Pensón che i morti del Vajónt[1] i é 'l dopio
de quei che ti tu à fat ades, ti tera.
Quant granda 'lora, póla esser la colpa
nostra? Si pur la pi gran colpa tóa,
tera, no l'é de 'verne fat noi, òmi.

Ma no stón dir cussì, proón a darse cór,
a indegnarse mèjo. E anca se sarà
una busia de pi, un inbrójo de pi,
aver pensà de fàrghela
contro tut quel che ne sta schifoso dentro
e ne fa zhavariar,
contro tut quel che ne sta atorno
nemigo imenso e scur
che da sote da sora da partut
ne vien ados, almanco no 'varón
barà inte 'l nostro dógo, contra noaltri stessi.
Pensón che quela testa santa

ne era complice, invece.
Pensiamo che i morti del Vajont sono il doppio
di quelli che tu hai fatto adesso, tu terra.
Quanto grande può essere dunque la nostra colpa?
Seppure la più grande tua colpa,
terra, non è quella di avere fatto noi, uomini.

Ma non diciamo così, proviamo a farci coraggio,
a meglio ingegnarci. E anche se sarà
ancora una menzogna, ancora un imbroglio,
aver pensato di farcela
contro tutto quello che di schifoso ci sta dentro
e ci fa delirare,
contro tutto quello che ci sta attorno
nemico immenso e oscuro
che da sotto da sopra da dovunque
ci viene addosso, almeno non avremo
barato nel nostro gioco, contro noi stessi.
Pensiamo che quella testa santa

and protect you against them, made dirty deals instead.
We think the dead of Vajont come to double
the number of those you've killed now, you, earth.
How great then could our fault be?
Even though, earth, your worst mistake
is not in having made us, men.

But let's not talk like that, let's try
to pluck up our courage, and really get going.
And even if it turns out to be another lie, another swindle,
to have thought of pulling it off
against everything lousy inside us
everything that makes us crazy,
against everything surrounding us
hostile immense and hidden
that from below from above from everywhere
strikes at us, at least we won't
have cheated in our game against ourselves.
Let's think that that sacred head

1. Even if the combination of the two tragedies may appear improper, it is certain that Vajont must be attributed in large measure to human error. Not to be forgotten. *T.N.*: A town in the Alto-Adige region of northern Italy, Vajont was largely destroyed when a dam broke on October 10, 1963, killing over two thousand people.

onipotente e misera—
boca che (no) parla, réce che (no) sente
mente che (no) pensa divinamente—
fursi la à sol bisòin che la jutóne 'n póch
che se jutóne 'n póch,
par esser tuta splendor, tuta ajuto.
E se i nostri voler insenbradi
e par éla e par noi 'ndarà avanti a capirla, a capirse,
no la ne falarà,
no la ne cascarà via da le man
inte i bojón che inciuca-dó e brusa/stusa,
la tirarón su tuta dal só mistero,
e si no tuta
—che no 'l saràe mai cont che torna just—
quel che basta parché
i só oci de bissa
de basilissa[1]
un póch in ne pare de vera
mama, no de marégna, no de bissa:
anca si Basilissa, Rèitia,[2] Dia

onnipotente e misera—
bocca che (non) parla, orecchi che (non) sentono
mente che (non) pensa divinamente—
forse ha solo bisogno che l'aiutiamo un poco,
che ci aiutiamo un poco,
per essere tutta splendore, tutta aiuto.
E se le nostre volontà unite
e per lei e per noi avanzeranno nel capirla, nel capirci,
non ci sfuggirà,
non ci cadrà via di mano
nei gorghi che inghiottono e bruciano/spengono,
la tireremo su intera dal suo mistero,
e se non tutta
—mai non sarebbe conto che torna giusto—
quanto basta perché
i suoi occhi di biscia
di sovrana
ci appaiano un poco di vera
mamma, non di matrigna, non di biscia:
anche se Basilissa, Rèitia, Dea

omnipotent and shabby—
mouth that does (does not) speak, ears that do (do not) hear
mind that does (does not) think divinely—
maybe only needs us to help it a little,
we need help each other a little,
for the head to become all brightness, all protection.
And if all our united wills/desires
for her and for us advance in understanding her, in understanding ourselves,
she won't escape us,
she won't drop from our hands
into the engulfing whirlpools that burn and blow out,
we'll get her up whole from her mystery,
and if not all of her
—nothing's perfect in this world—
as much as we need so that
her eyes of a snake
of a sovereign
appear to us a little like
those of a true mama, not a stepmother, not a snake:
even if Basilissa, Rèitia, Goddess

1. *Basilissa*: see the second strophe of "Venetian Recitative."

2. Rèitia is the principal divinity, feminine, of the paleo-Veneto. *T.N.*: See the note to the epigraph of "Venetian Recitative."

(fursi che spèta un sposo tant eterno
cofà éla—e che l'é éla—, Λόγος ἐρχόμενος)[1]
l'à da restar: par al nostro no-saver
e saver, ma pi de tut pa'l nostro amarla.

• • •

Vecio parlar che tu à inte 'l tó saór
un s'cip del lat de la Eva,
vecio parlar che no so pi,
che me se á descuní
dì par dì 'nte la boca (e no tu me basta);
che tu sé canbià co la me fazha
co la me pèl ano par an;
parlar porét, da poreti, ma s'cèt
ma fis, ma tóch cofà 'na branca
de fien 'pena segà dal faldin (parché no bàstetu?)—
noni e pupà i é 'ndati, quei che te cognosséa,
none e mame le é 'ndate, quele che te inventéa,
nóvo petèl par ogni fiól in fasse,
intra le strússie, i zhighi dei part, la fan e i afanézh.

(forse che aspetta uno sposo eterno
come lei—e che è lei—, Logos veniente)
deve restare; per il nostro non-sapere
e sapere, ma soprattutto per il nostro amarla.

• • •

Vecchio dialetto che hai nel tuo sapore
un gocciolo del latte di Eva,
vecchio dialetto che non so più,
che mi ti sei estenuato
giorno per giorno nella bocca (e non mi basti);
che sei cambiato con la mia faccia
con la mia pelle anno per anno;
parlare povero, da poveri, ma schietto
ma fitto, ma denso come una manciata
di fieno appena tagliato dalla falce (perché non basti?)—
nonni e babbi sono andati, loro che ti conoscevano,
nonne e mamme sono andate, loro che ti inventavano
nuovo petèl per ogni figlio in fasce
tra gli stenti, le grida di parto, la fame, le nausee.

(who waits perhaps for a bridegroom
eternal like her—and that is her—, *logos erchomenos*)
she must remain; for our not-knowing
and knowing, but above all, for our loving her.

• • •

Ancient dialect, your flavor still has
a drop of Eve's milk,
ancient dialect that I've forgotten,
you've worn yourself out
day by day in my mouth (and you're not enough for me);
you've changed with my face
with my hide year after year;
poor speech, of poor folks, but you're pure,
thick and dense as a handful
of hay freshly cut with the scythe (why aren't you enough?)—
grandpas and dads have died, they're the ones who used to know you,
grandmas and mamas have died, they who made up for you
new baby-talk for every baby in diapers,
in the suffering, the screams of labor, the hunger, the nausea.

1. "The coming logos."

Girar me fa fastidi, in médo a 'ste masiére
de ti, de mi. Dal dent cagnin del tenp
inte 'l piat sivanzhi no ghén resta, e manco
de tut i zhimiteri: òe da dirte zhimitero?
Élo vero che pi no pól esserghe 'romai
gnessun parlar de néne[1]-none-mame? Che fa mal
ai fiói 'l petèl e i gran mestri lo sconsilia?
Élo vero che scriverte,
parlar vecio, l'é massa un sforzh, l'é un mal
anca par mi, cofà ciór par revèrs,
par straòlt, far 'ndar fora le corde de le man?
Ma intant, qua par atorno, a girar pa'i marcà,
o mèjo a 'ndar par canp e rive e zhópe[2]
là onde che 'l gal de cristal canta senpre tre òlte,
da juste boche se te sent. Mi ò pers la trazha,
lontan massa son 'ndat pur stando qua
invidà, inbulonà, deventà squasi un zhóch de pionbo,
e la poesia no l'é in gnessuna lengua
in gnessun logo—fursi—o l'é 'l busnar del fógo
che 'l fa screcolar tute le fonde

Girare mi dà fastidio, in mezzo a queste macerie
di te, di me. Dal dente accanito del tempo
avanzi non restano nel piatto, e meno
di tutto i cimiteri: devo dirti cimitero?
È vero che non può esserci più ormai
nessun parlare di néne-nonne-mamme? Che fa male
ai bambini il petèl e gran maestri lo sconsigliano?
È vero che scriverti,
vecchio parlare, è troppo faticoso, è un male
anche per me, come prendere a rovescio,
per obliquo, far slogare i tendini delle mani?
Ma intanto qui attorno, girando per i mercati,
o meglio andando per campi e clivi e balze
là dove il gallo di cristallo canta sempre tre volte,
da giuste bocche ti si sente. Io ho perduto la traccia,
sono andato troppo lontano pur rimanendo qui
avvitato, imbullonato, diventato quasi un ceppo di piombo,
e la poesia non è in nessuna lingua
in nessun luogo—forse—o è il rugghiare del fuoco
che fa scricchiolare tutte le fondamenta

Poking around in this rubble—yours and mine—bothers me.
Nothing's left on the plate
thanks to the fierce eye-tooth of time,
and even less of the graveyards: should I call you graveyard?
Is it true these days there can't be any more
a speech for godmothers-grandmas-mamas?
Does baby-talk hurt children and do the big experts advise against it?
Is it true that writing you, old speech,
is too tiring, is it a pain even for me,
the way grabbing something from the wrong side,
from the wrong angle, dislocates the hand's tendons?
Meanwhile, in these parts, visiting the markets,
or better yet, walking the fields, the hills and cliffs,
where the crystal rooster always crows three times,
we hear you spoken by upright mouths. I've lost track,
I've gone too far while staying here
screwed down, bolted in, having become almost a block of lead,
and poetry's not in any language
in any place—maybe—or it's the crackling of fire
that makes all the foundations creak

1. *Néne* means literally "wet nurses" but here it indicates the by now nonexistent gentle little women of the entourage.
2. *Zhópe*: the word means "clod" as much as "cliff."

inte la gran laguna, inte la gran lacuna—
la é 'l pien e 'l vódo dela testa-tera
che tas, o zhigna e usma un pas pi in là
de quel che mai se podaràe dirse, far nostro.
Ma ti, vecio parlar, resisti. E si anca i òmi
te desmentegarà senzha inacòrderse,
ghén sarà osèi—
do tre osèi sói magari
dai sbari e dal mazhelo zoladi via—:
doman su l'ultima rama là in cao
in cao de zhiése e pra,
osèi che te à inparà da tant
te parlarà inte 'l sol, inte l'onbría.

L'ora se slanguoris inte 'l zhendre del scaldin,
l'é l'ora de des'ciorse, de assar al calduzh, al coàt.
Ma da 'ste póche brónzhe de qua dó,
dai fià dei filò de qua dó,
si i fii, si i fii
del insoniarse e rajonar tra lori se filarà,
là sù, là par atorno del ventar de le stele
se inpizharà i nostri mili parlar e pensar nóvi
inte 'n parlar che sarà un par tuti,
fondo come un basar,

dentro la grande laguna, dentro la grande lacuna—
è il pieno e il vuoto della testa-terra
che tace, o ammicca e fiuta un passo più oltre
di quel che mai potremmo dirci, far nostro.
Ma tu, vecchio parlare, persisti. E seppur gli uomini
ti dimenticheranno senza accorgersene,
ci saranno uccelli—
due tre uccelli soltanto magari
dagli spari e dal massacro volati via—:
domani sull'ultimo ramo là in fondo
in fondo a siepi e prati,
uccelli che ti hanno appreso da tanto tempo,
ti parleranno dentro il sole, nell'ombra.

L'ora illanguidisce nella cenere dello scaldino,
è l'ora di andarsene, di lasciare il calduccio del covo.
Ma dalle poche braci di quaggiù,
dai fiati dei filò di quaggiù,
se i fili, se i fili
del sogno e della ragione tra loro si fileranno,
lassù, nei dintorni del tirar vento di stelle
si accenderanno i nostri mille parlari e pensieri nuovi
in un parlare che sarà uno per tutti,
fondo come un baciare,

in the great laguna, in the great lacuna—
it's the fullness and the void of the earth-Mother
who keeps silent, or winks and sniffs out a track further on,
one that we could never name or make our own.
But you, ancient tongue, endure! And even if people
will someday forget you without noticing it,
there'll be birds—
maybe only two or three birds
who will have flown away from the shooting and the killing—:
tomorrow on the last branch way down there
at the end of thickets and of meadows,
birds who learned you long ago,
they'll speak you in sunshine, and in shadows.

The hour is dying down in the ashes of the warming-pan,
it's time to go, to leave the warmth of the shelter.
But from the few embers down here,
from the breaths of the peasants wake down here,
if the threads, if the threads
of dreaming and thinking spin themselves together,
up there, where winds blow gusting stars,
our thousand tongues and new thoughts will kindle
in a dialect that will be one for everybody,
deep as kissing,

vèrt sul ciaro, sul scur,
davanti la manèra inpiantada inte 'l scur
col só taj ciaro, 'pena guà da senpre.

(Disèe manèra, disèe taj,
e l'era sol che 'na sguinzhada
un jozholar de débol miel
de lustri mèsteghi de bròse e guazh.)
(Disèe fii, disèe fià,
e co le ónge intive sol che in
s'césene—noi—de calcossa
desconpagnà   sparpagnà
inte la lópa de un posterno[1]   eterno)
(Disèe, disèe   )

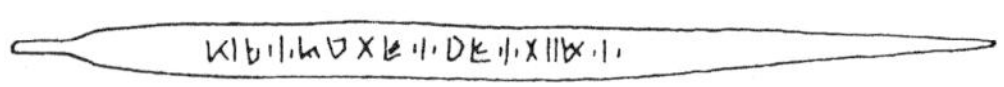

('Note, 'note; 'l filó l'é finí)

luglio–ottobre 1976

aperto sulla luce, sul buio,
davanti la mannaia piantata nel buio
col suo taglio chiaro, appena affilato da sempre.

(Dicevo mannaia, dicevo taglio
ed era solo uno sprizzare
un gocciolare di debole miele
di miti luci di brine e rugiade.)
(Dicevo fili, dicevo fiati,
e con le unghie incappo solo in
schegge—noi—di qualcosa
scompaginato   sparpagliato
nel muschio di un a-nord   eterno)
(Dicevo dicevo   )

[A RÈITIA SANATRICE]

(Buona notte, buona notte, il filò è terminato)

luglio–ottobre 1976

open onto the light, onto the dark,
in front of the great axe fixed firmly in the darkness
with its bright blade, newly sharpened forever.

  (I said an axe, I said a blade
and it was only a sprinkle
  a dribble of mild honey
of faint lights of frosts and dews.)
    (I said threads, breaths,
    and with my fingernails I run into
    only splinters—us—of something
    discombobulated   scattered
    in the moss of an a-North   eternal)
(I was saying, I started to say   )

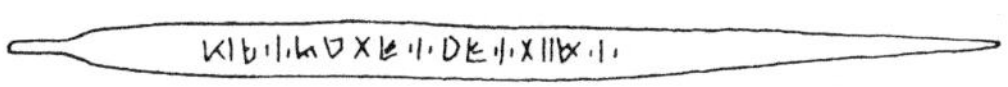

(Good night, good night now; the peasants wake is finished)

July–October 1976

1. "A-North": the part facing north, in shadow, of buildings (and also of places).

Observations on the Meaning and the Situation of the Dialects in Italy in the Late Twentieth Century

The first two compositions in this volume I had already written, to some degree. They existed scattered through my works of many, even very many, years ago. Of course, not in this precise form, which is one of the many possible for an insistent theme, never completely expressible, almost ubiquitous today. However, I owe the encounter with this incarnation of the theme, which the occasion required in dialectal words, to the mystical and humoral arrogance of the colors and images, to the realities and to the oneiric traffic jams out of which Federico Fellini has woven this film of his, pursuing Casanova's unpredictability through his own. There remained, and remains, for me the uncertainty of "dialect," of its particularly treacherous chess-board. But aside from the fact that the Veneto dialect is (was) a powerful language, capable also of originating an equally valid and complex literature, has there ever truly existed a dialect that was not something explosively different, at least potentially, however much the term itself, with its implied reductiveness, proposes? Moreover, today less than ever do we know what *dialects* are, in their infinitesimal capillary movements, and what *languages* are, especially those tending toward a panterrestrial diffusion, nor how their destinies intersect. In this case, Fellini's visual discourse awoke in me a variety of resonances within a certain linguistic aura to be called of the Veneto (Venetian only in part) both by excess and by lack. I came upon a way of speaking lost in the diachrony and in the synchrony of the Veneto, up to the paradox and the unreality of a paleo-Venetic quotation, a way of speaking partly invented, partly imitated from excessively high models, in which apprehension for the rights of glottology and philology could not hold at bay the desire to tear up the margins, to go far away, to "run off the road." Of course, along the line sketched by Federico Fellini in his fertile and generous letter, one could have done more and better, aside from the limits of space posed by the film's situations.

And I am grateful to Fellini for having pushed me gently, winking and almost signaling silence with a finger to his lips, to this brief, but for me not negligible, descent by very precipitous shortcuts, often glimpsed, but never exactly frequented previously here and in this manner: with an eye on many goddesses, from the Head, to Rèitia, to Venice, to the Giantess doll: all reducible to a single reality, even in the immense remoteness of their icons, their meanings, their times.

• • •

Along this itinerary was born a meditation, or better a "second discourse," "Peasants Wake," which required of me the almost metalinguistic use (in a situation obscurely constrictive) of the dialect of the places/place where I was born and have always lived.

The dialect used in "Peasants Wake" is approximately that which is still spoken in the valley of the Soligo (upper Trevisan), with different nuances for words, idiomatic expressions, inflections; which, as always, refer to narrow fringes of classes, minimal groups, single localities. In this way, for example, there coexist *se* and *si* (more rural) for *se,* and *come, 'fa, cofà* (the now rare *comódo*) for *come.* Analogously *noi* will be found more in Soligo than in Pieve, while the "*th*" (rendered as *zh*) varies greatly and is more marked the more one moves away from the centers of the villages. And if certain words will appear to today's reader to be almost the result of a restoration (for example, *fursi* for *forse*), this is due to the fact that I continue to have in my ear the dialect that was spoken in my early childhood in the *Cal Santa* quarter inhabited by common people; and which, of course, was much more characteristic, above all due to the abundance of original idiomatic expressions. But it is necessary to recognize that the present speech is less eroded than it might appear at first sight; there exist true words of today, such as *inbulonà* and the like, fully integrated to the interior of a rhythm of self-preservation and indeed of enrichment, under certain aspects. It is a sign of vitality, somewhat stunned, "on the edge," thin and intense as a trickle of blood.

Certain syntactical violations, certain morphological simplifications or lexical trimmings, are very evident in these writings, but not so much as to change the nature of the whole. Dialect, all things considered, is an absolute freedom, capable of tracing consistent/mutable limits.

But what can a humble dialect (very distant even from the illustrious vernacular of the Veneto and its literary examples), above all for those who have always spoken it and feel it disappearing from their mouths, "from beneath" every intention, mean today? It is, in any case, the standard, tragically blurred for this lifetime, in which all that is unstable, ephemeral, uncertain, presents itself. It is the story of a deafening and a silencing imposed from the outside in a way more insidious than witchcraft. Nor does this actually come about through the compensating force of a great language (great culture) that could have given the impression of being such (and in part was) a downright illustrious and monumental Italian, which imposed itself *after* the dialect, or rather, superimposed itself on it, leaving it practically unharmed, on the whole.

Dialect, at any rate, for those who have found themselves speaking it alongside the language, in a kind of almost repressed diglossia, poses itself like a "first mystery," which escapes every possible contemplation as well as every objectifying detachment. It is a situation that involves a remarkable number of Italians, even if in different forms and degree, and which statistics say is minutely variable from year to year.

These experiences are lacking in those who belong to that extensive group that knows, well or poorly, only the language (but "which one," then?); while at the polar-opposite deprivation, and with much greater danger, are those who, knowing only the spoken dialect, remain, literally, "foreclosed." Semi-incompetent competency, performance that is almost not perceived as such, authentic means of contrast with respect to the luminous and hyperconscious phenomena that occur in "speaking a language," dialect appears as the metaphor—and it is, from a certain angle, the reality—of every excess, unimaginability, gushing effusion or ambiguous stagnancy of the linguistic fact in its most profound nature. It remains laden with the vertigo of the past, of the megacenturies in which it extended, infiltrated, subdivided, recomposed itself, in which "the" language died and was reborn (song, rhythm, dancing muscles, dream, reason, functionality) within a very violent drift that causes us to tremble with uneasiness because there we *touch,* with the tongue (in its two meanings of physical organ and word-system), our lack of knowledge from whence speech comes, and, in the moment in which it comes, rises like milk: in perfect opposition, here, to the other language, that "high one," valuable (at least apparently) as a distinct lexical and morphosyntactic totality, disposed to undergo use and maneuverings—while the lower current of the spoken dialect "makes do." It is the experimentation of an orality (zone of nourishment, "phase," etc.), an oracle-arity, an oratory, minimal yet fortified with all the viscosity that permeates it, reconnecting it directly to all the environmental, biological, "cosmic" contexts, liberating *within* them the desire for expression and expression itself. Dialect is felt as coming from a place where no writing exists (the one which is only thousands of years old) nor "grammar": the location, therefore, of a logos that remains always *erchómenos,** which never freezes in a slice of event, which remains almost infantile even in its speaking, which, at any rate, is far from every throne. Poured back again into the earth, connected/disconnected in such "humility," this logos speaks through the thousand mouths of the "lowly," and, in any case, in the millions of "errors," of individual wanderings, highly mysterious rebels, in which the canons of yesterday and of today are consumed, and those of tomorrow are concealed: but just from being, in some way, rendered comic from the start. Dialect announces itself as the vague site in which *langue* and *parole* tend to identify themselves, and every territoriality vanishes into those that are contiguous.

And here would begin, with particularly deep emotion, a discussion of the Neo-Latin situation, on the whirlpool from the bottom of which (with relative distortion in the perpetual orality) Latin is the object, the arch-language, arch-engraved on commemorative tables, the imperial and definitive language: but doubled in addition by one of its very fresh anti-institutional vernaculars. And we would need to mention the twists and turns, rebirths, metamorphoses, *splittings*† of every kind proper to the Neo-Latin linguistic area and perhaps not findable in a form so dazzling and significant in another area.

For this reason, for the "semi-diglossic person" who "sees double" and speaks on a double track of systems, very close in

* *T.N.: Coming*

† *T.N.:* In English in the original.

general, but wide apart in their destination, it must be frightening to *write* the dialect that leads the game although "feeling" relatively deficient with respect to the language and that permeates in its being ("wanting to be?") pulsation and somatic gurgling: of a continuum and of changing pluriformities, similar to those of life, sunk in it and at the same time floating on its upper limits, toward symbol. There remains, moreover, the enormous diversity of motivations of the individual dialect authors, especially today, and how much in them is hidden.

Dialectality, nevertheless, for centuries had guaranteed a certain comfortable and implicit feeling of cohesion and duration, even though within narrow limits and according to the degrees of knowledge and lack of knowledge of the speakers. At present, its nature, minute-fluid-interreticular and, above all, averse to the rigidity of the "national" reticules, its nature as an unconscious that, precisely, "explodes" slowly, reveals itself exactly in the moment when the source of orality itself is threatened, and every unconscious, every "maternality," risks being erased. On the other side, the national language is in danger of becoming bloodless, amorphous, riddled with stereotypes and video-bureaucratic waste just at the moment in which it becomes popular: but late, and when it already seems somewhat useless because spoken in an increasingly narrow area (with respect to the other major languages), and therefore "debased" in its turn to the level of a dialect but without having certain undefinable faculties of adaptation that dialect has. Therefore, the situation of the Italian speaker and writer is one of the most precarious, distressing, insane. Genocide breathes around and inside it, even if still in a minor key.

To sacrifice oneself to a moment that is of rituality/clash patrolling the dialect sites and writing-describing them with an inevitable effect of distortion and "indetermination" appears justified even if we don't know how productive. It remains bound, in any case, to an attitude that can only be outside of "this" time, precisely because it has ventured into a time of different directions and *durée;* and for this it has to do almost solely with poetry, rarely with prose (understood in their most obvious and necessary meanings). But for this reason the contact with dialects, killed but never dead, pinpoint in form but with linkages and echoes in the most incredible distances, is capable of framing, even if in encrypted terms, the most dazzling opening onto alterities, futures, active dissolvings. Dialect can have nothing to do with re-exhumations or embalmments "as on the reservation." It must be felt as a guide—beyond any hypothesis whatsoever concerning its destiny—to single out the signs of new realities that are pressing to emerge.

Orthographic Note

The orthography, which follows the Italian to the greatest degree possible, tends to adhere to a "mean" tradition, so to speak, mean or average, that is, with respect to the codes that vary, obviously, from author to author. I have indicated the "acute" or "grave" accents on *e* and *o* for phonetic precision where the Veneto word bore no similarity to the corresponding Italian, or where, even though a similarity existed, the pronunciation of the vowel was different.

Since it is natural in the Veneto dialect to truncate words that end in a consonant, the relative accents have been omitted, except in some instances in which they contributed to clarifying values of meaning or of rhythm. Instead, I have indicated the accent in words ending with a consonant but not truncated.

S represents unvoiced *s* at the beginning and at the end of a word, and voiced *s* within a word (with the exception of instances in which the grouping with other consonants requires a different pronunciation, as in Italian).

SS represents the normal unvoiced *s* within a word even though in many instances the pronunciation is so marked that it comes very close to the double *s*.

Z represents voiced *s* at the beginning of a word, or intermediate sounds between voiced *z* and voiced *s* within a word; *s'c* is the union of unvoiced *s* and soft *c*.

In texts like the ones presented here, the pronunciation of *l* varies greatly. It is marked, if meant to be rendered in the archaic manner. It can be weak or fading, closely approaching the modern *l*, or, even "effaced" as in the *petèl* (the language of infants) that appears in "London Lullaby." There remains, analogously, a certain interchangeability in the pronunciation of the two letters *j* and *g*, usually clearly differentiated.

Zh is meant to represent the current, most common pronunciation of the "th" sound, which, even though today it is losing its original force, has not, however, approached unvoiced *z*. The possible *dh* has been allowed to disappear, and is commonly reduced to *d*.

From *Idioma*

Idiom

Gente—come tante altre genti—
. . . .
  Forse è per questo che ho sempre stentato
  e malvoluto partire,
  per l'invadenza beata di una certa tua virtù
  che in nonviolenza tesse
  e ritesse quotidianità—
  essa di per sé dona tanti altri beni
  di accoglienza e dolcezza
  reciproca, né esclude la fermezza—
    pur se tra lievi distrazioni
    reciproche, indifferenze incrociate
    coaguli di minimi affari e mafie—
    e poi una piccola appiccicosa
    volontà di non guardar troppo lontano
    una bonarietà qualche volta sonnolenta

Mi scopro talvolta del tutto solo
pensando a tali cose, sento di
omettere molto, di non poter
né saper dire di più,
ma poi mi libero,
con un po' di sgomento un po' di gioia
che ‖ e mi adagio nel giusto

Peoples

People—like so many other peoples—
. . . .
  Perhaps that's why I've always found it hard
  and been reluctant to leave,
  for the blessed intrusiveness of a certain virtue of yours
  that in nonviolence weaves
  and reweaves daily reality—
  in itself it brings so many other good things
  acceptance and reciprocal sweetness,
  nor does it exclude firmness—
    even if among light reciprocal distractions,
    interwoven indifferences,
    coagulants of minimal affairs and mafias—
    and then a small sticky
    determination not to look too far into the distance
    a sometimes drowsy goodness

At times I find myself completely alone
thinking about such things, I feel
I'm leaving out a lot, that I don't know
how to say more,
but then I break free,
with a bit of dismay a bit of joy
that || and I relax in the right

essere uno coi tanti di qui.
Mi libero: e vedo una carta che va
verso nord, nel vento, verso la notte.

E talvolta mi abbacina un prato
dimenticato dietro una casa antica,
solitario, che finge indifferenza o
lieve o smunta distrazione

ma forse soffre, forse è soltanto
un paradiso

being one with so many here.
I break free: and I see a piece of paper going
toward the north, in the wind, toward the night.

At times a meadow dazzles me
forgotten behind an ancient house,
solitary, feigning indifference or
slight or pale distraction

        but maybe it's suffering, maybe it's only
                a paradise

Sfere

Come di là dai mari
grida grida l'innocenza—
bambini non più solitari
su litorali infiniti
rincorrono rincorrono e vincono
di abbaglio in abbaglio rapiti

E che si saprà mai di tanta innocenza?
Che di questo spisciarsi di bambini?
Feroci come l'afa
come i divini
loro doni che fuggono, sfere
su tutto il mondo, oltre ogni potere?

Folla che troppo distratto e assonnato
raggiungo ad una svolta
a un dirupo dove crollò improvviso
ogni confine in un soprassaltante riso,
    folla dolcissima, vero
    disumano, perfetto aldilà
    in elisie Tivù, fosfeni a cascate,
    acufeni di gloria gloria e gloria
        per questa bella estate.

Spheres

As if beyond the seas
innocence cries out, cries out—
children no longer solitary
on never-ending shores
give chase, give chase and vanquish
transported from gleam to gleam

And what will we ever know of such innocence?
Of this great outpouring of children?
Fierce as sultry weather
as their divine gifts
that flee, spheres
all over the world, beyond every power?

Crowd that, overly distraught and drowsy,
I join at a curve
at a precipice where suddenly
every boundary crashed in an overwhelming laugh,
    sweet crowd, truly
    dishuman, perfect kingdom-come
    in TV Elysiums, phosphenes cascading,
    acouphenes of glory glory and more glory
        for this beautiful summer.

Orizzonti

Stanco di non allinearmi
verso l'orizzontalità—e con odio
dell'irrequietezza dei colli,
stanco forse di avervi insultati
accettando che diveniste fantasmi,
o genitori:
che pressoché dissonate, che state fuori
da ogni contaminazione o sospetto
o lecca-lecca di tempo,
fuori dagli effetti speciali
e dai metabolismi erratici
del Tutto. Non avete bisogno
del mio sostegno, del mio
ricordo.
Non esiste bisogno né critica del bisogno.
Siamo, anche se io stento, fatti di orizzonte,
disadattati a questo tipo di mondo.
Ma in linea di massima convinti
    (costituendo chissà quale frase)
    di essere,
    di meritarci di essere, un bell'essere,

Horizons

Tired of not aligning myself
toward horizonality—and with hatred
of the hills' restlessness,
tired perhaps of having insulted you
accepting your having become ghosts,
oh parents:
who are almost discordant, beyond
every contamination or suspicion
or time's eternal lapping,
outside of special effects
and erratic metabolisms
of the All. You don't need
my support, my
recollection.
Need does not exist, nor criticism of need.
We are, even if I find it difficult, made of horizon,
unadapted to this kind of world.
But on the whole convinced
    (constituting who knows what sentence)
    of being,
    of deserving to be, a fine being,

di avere in pugno, chissà come,
ogni carenza e rastrematura
infida e terrificante
                    dell'essere.

to have in hand, who knows how,
every privation and diminution
treacherous and terrifying
of being.

VORREI SAPERLO

Arte imparata, mettila da parte.
Se volete sapere dove c'è vino buono,
in quale osteria o casa di contadini
con la rama per insegna, rivolgetevi
alla Nene. Ottantacinque segna il suo calendario.
Vive, bene e ben sola, nella casetta in Cal Santa.
Io scrivevo sui muri della Cal Santa
—e un occhio mistico e callido lo può leggere ancora
al di là dell'usura, forse lo scoprirà domani—
"Nene dictatrice in hoc vico, MCMXXXIX."
Quest'anno ha rinnovato i soffitti,
l'altr'anno ha colorato le imposte,
Un Signore chiamò la sua cucina: oasi di pace.
Voleva trasformare la sua poltrona in pollaio
e la scaletta da fiori in armadio. Nella cucina
la sveglia ha una civile maestà nel ticchettio
per cui l'eterno vige, su quel pavimento di cotto,
tra quelle pareti a calce, col tavolo, l'uovo e il buon bicchiere.
Critica i programmi della radio.
Va a letto alle sette ora ch'è inverno
e impietra il ciel di Cal Santa la tramontana. Ma:
Nene indovina dov'è il vino più fine.
Le sue passeggiate si perdono dietro le colline.
D'estate gira per casa in camicia, e così la sorprese

I WOULD LIKE TO KNOW

Learning—put it aside.
If you want to know where to find good wine,
in which tavern or peasants' house
with the branch as sign, talk to
Nene. Her calendar marks eighty-five.
She lives well and very alone in the little house in Cal Santa.
I wrote on the walls of Cal Santa
—and a mystical and astute eye can still read it
beyond the wear and tear, maybe discover it tomorrow—
"Nene dictatrice in hoc vico, MCMXXXIX."
This year she renovated the ceilings,
last year she painted the shutters,
A Gentleman called her kitchen: peaceful oasis.
She wanted to transform her easy-chair into a hen-roost
and the flowered ladder into a cupboard. In the kitchen
the alarm clock has a refined majesty in its ticking
by which the eternal remains in force, above that brickwork floor,
between those whitewashed walls, with the table, the egg, and the good glass of wine.
She criticizes the radio programs.
She goes to bed at seven now that it's winter
and the sky of Cal Santa turns to stone at sundown. But:
Nene foretells where the best wine is to be found.
Her walks get lost behind the hills.
In the summer she waltzes around the house in a nightgown,

una volta il cappellano andando a questua.
Se ne parlò durante il grande passato,
quello nostro, con nevi e soli d'antan
e ghiaie ed erbe-diamantine
su cui faticavano coi piedini i fratellini Pomo e Scorza,
chiamati di favola in favola
a distrarci dai singulti, in grazia della Nene.
Farà, in futuro, forte d'intonaci tutta la casa,
renderà, forse, moderno
il portichetto eccetera che dà sull'aperto.
Si sveglia di notte e dice molte e molte preghiere
per chi—racconta—è dimenticato da tutti
e/o per chi dimentica di pregare. Canta, certe volte.
Si hanno registrazioni
del suo bel-modulato "Casta diva,"
non tremola che poco. Ride un poco
di sé, ma più in sé crede.
I tempi dell'oasi di pace. Spazi, pavimenti,
obbietti, sentenze. Tempi
che ancora esistete v'ispessite arricchite
dolcemente cumulate in voi stessi—
espunti o imperliti
anche i più minuscoli bruscoli di mali.
Ah gl'incendi tedeschi del '44

and that's how she was surprised once by the chaplain making his pastoral visit.
We talked about it during the great bygone days,
our own, with suns and snows of yesteryear
            and pebbles and adamantine-grasses
on which the Pomo and Scorza brothers toiled with their small feet,
called from fable to fable
to distract us from the hiccups, with Nene's help.
She will fortify the whole house, in the future, with whitewash,
maybe modernize
the little porch etcetera that opens onto the outside.
She wakes up at night and says prayer after prayer
for those—as she says—forgotten by everyone,
and/or for those who forget to pray. She sings, sometimes.
We have recordings
of her finely modulated "Casta diva,"
with only a few tremolos. She laughs a little
at herself, but believes in herself even more.
The times of the peaceful oasis. Spaces, floors,
objects, sayings. Times
that still exist, you thicken enrich
sweetly accumulate in yourselves—
having vanquished or adorned
even the tiniest specks of misfortunes.
Oh the German fires of '44

Ah la cometa del '56 nel cielo freddo-estivo
Ah la gallinella dileguata,
la pannocchia rubata,
le scurette occultate dai ragazzacci.
Ah l'uovo e il bicchiere di rosso. Tu temi? Tu temi?
Così immediato è qui l'eterno, così
tangibile frutto del tempo, suo qualitativo
lucore, così in saliente colloquio.
E così falso ogni sospetto
su cose e parvenze. Che qui non passano mai
come non passano le loro cause e ragioni perfette.

Oh the comet of '56 in the summer-cold sky
Oh the little hen that vanished,
the stolen corncob,
the hatchets hidden by the naughty boys.
Oh the egg and the glass of red wine. Are you afraid? Are you afraid?
Here the eternal is so immediate, such
tangible fruit of time, its qualitative
brilliance, in such salient colloquy.
And so false all suspicion
about things and appearances. That never pass by here
just as their causes and perfect reasons don't pass by.

NINO NEGLI ANNI OTTANTA

25 gennaio 1983, S. Paolo

Durante l'estate sotto l'equivoco sudore
del solstizio arrancavi
Nino, come reggendoti a malapena
sulla sponda dell'aldiquà,
salivi le chine incretinite
del tuo feudo ormai scalpato
            d'ogni vite,
dai grevi tacchini sbeccuzzato
vedovo di lepri e fagiani, strampalato.
    Tu faticavi, vestito di nero, ansimavi
la tua già irreale presenza
anche se egregiamente
raccordato a fermezze finezze
imprinting elementi
per ogni dove a noi da sempre sfuggenti.
    Ora no: splende ora gennaio
    e la gloria di gennaio ti assume
                        a sé—
immune da malattie
svelto del tuo costume,   privo
dei defedanti soprabiti.
E certo la tua fronte può di ghiaccioli

NINO IN THE EIGHTIES

January 25, 1983, the Feast of St. Paul

During the summer under the equivocal sweat
of the solstice you were trudging along,
Nino, barely staying upright
on the bank of the here-and-now,
you were climbing the slopes without meaning
of your fiefdom now scalped
            of every vine,
pecked at by fat turkeys,
widower of hares and pheasants, eccentric.
      You toiled, dressed in black, panting,
your already unreal presence
even if eminently
connected to steadiness shrewdness
imprinting elements
everywhere, always escaping us.
      Now, not so: now January shines
      and January's glory takes you
                              to itself—
immune from illnesses
agile in your usual way,   lacking
protective overcoats.
And of course your forehead can make itself

farsi scintillante com'è di quotidianità
        e di furbizia contro l'aldilà,
quando, pedalando
tra i novanta e i cento anni quasi volage,
ti addentri nel mistero delle colline
per te ricanticchiato, riacutizzato senza fine.

sparkle with icicles since it's made of daily reality
        and with cunning against the beyond,
when, pedaling
between ninety and one hundred years, almost flighty,
you penetrate the mystery of the hills
for you sung softly again, made keen again, without end.

ANDAR A CUCIRE

A la Maria Carpèla
(che la 'ndéa a pontar par le case)

Si no 'l te fèsse 'n paradiso
aposta par ti, anca si paradisi no ghe n'é,
al saràe da méter a l'inferno
l'istesso Padreterno—
la saràe da méter a l'inferno
tuta, tuta quanta "la realtà,"
si par ti no la fèsse 'n paradiso
pien de bontà come la tó bontà,
gnentaltro che 'l paradiso
come che ti tu l'à pensà.

A Maria Carpel
(che andava a cucire presso le famiglie)

Se non ti facesse un paradiso
apposta per te, anche se paradisi non ce ne sono,
sarebbe da mettere all'inferno
lo stesso Padre Eterno—
sarebbe da mettere all'inferno
tutta, tutta quanta la realtà,
se per te non facesse un paradiso
pieno di bontà come la tua bontà,
niente altro che il paradiso
come tu l'hai pensato.

La contrada. Zauberkraft.
Come è esistita la contrada? Si può
davvero assumerla come un dato—
o almeno un fattore di contestualità?
Lei con le casette male allineate
sbocconcellate ma talvolta
messe a nuovo dal vento
o da soldi arrivati col vento . . .
Sì, la tua esistenza
chiede, si attira lettere patenti, attestati

GOING OUT TO SEW

for Maria Carpèla
(who went out to do sewing for people)

If He didn't make a heaven
just for you, even if heavens don't exist,
the Eternal Father Himself
should be consigned to hell—
and all of Reality should go there too,
If He didn't make a heaven
full of goodness like your goodness,
nothing less than the heaven
pictured by you.

The quarter. Zauberkraft.
How did the quarter exist? Can we
really assume it as a given—
or at least a contextual fact?
She with her little houses poorly aligned
chipped but sometimes
made new by the wind
or by money blown in by the wind . . .
Yes, your existence
asks for, attracts letters of patent, witnessings

del resto superflui,
sta, a picco, su ciò che di per sé sprofonda
nella propria sovrana potenza
(potenza intesa come spessore del ghiaccio
    in una valle ampia, fatta a U
    ghiaccio mai sciolto, nonostante il parere dei più)
Occorre tutta la Zauberkraft
di cui parlava Hegel
come di cosa di cui lui sapeva qualcosa
per credere che la contrada senza posa
si rinnovi in face mentale, vibri
notte e dì stravolta da irti inesprimibili
soli, saggezze, tenebre, riposi e gridi-cigolii:
tela in cui
le stanzette in cui
le funzioni i grafemi in cui
i lucignoli gli smoccolii in cui
noi-io   ci risolvemmo
o magari in finissimo etra

Come si può pretendere
che qualcuno sopravviva con piccoli commerci
in precarietà più delicate che vapori sui vetri
che orgogli di fili d'erba, di aghi di brina:

however superfluous,
it stands perpendicular over that which sinks by itself
into its own sovereign power
(strength understood as the thickness of the ice
        in a wide valley, shaped like a U
        ice that never melted, despite the majority view)
We need the whole Zauberkraft
of which Hegel spoke
as of something he knew about
so as to believe that the quarter might be endlessly renewed
in intellectual light, it vibrates
night and day overcome by bristling inexpressible
suns, wisdoms, darkness, rests and shrieks-squeaks:
web in which
the little rooms where
the functions the graphemes in which
the wicks the snuffings in which
we-I   were transformed
or maybe into very fine ether

How can we insist
that somebody survives on small dealings
in precarious states more delicate than mists on windowpanes
than showy grassblades, or frost needles:

a te due castagne, io ti lavoro una sedia,
tu un materasso, io ti cucio un abitino
e io che faccio il contadino
        Occorre una Zauberkraft senza pari
per sperare di arrivare a domani, a dopodomani
così commerciando e dandosi a manipolare—
senza precipitar giù tra le nebulose
senza scivolare in un unico passo falso, di sette leghe
Tu non tornare alla decenza dello stato minerale
        Zauberkraft è la mia contrada
        l'edificio della mente non lo sento possibile
        l'illuminazione ottico-mentale
        funziona con orari incerti—mi sta imbrogliando
        Ma avallo, firmo cambiali
        su sentieri di Zauberkraft
        in stanzette di Zauberkraft
        pur senza picciòlo cordone tubetto di flebo;
        e per qualche arteriola—vedi—si riattiva il circolo
        balugina sempre l'anagrafe
Quanto   vi costò trattenervi
qua su in contrada a manipolare
e, per me già spinto a spallate dove   invade
quanta mania ci fu, contrada, per
reggerti, sola in tutta la tua siderale

to you two chestnuts, I'm working on your chair,
a mattress for you, I'm sewing a little suit
and it's I who plays the peasant
  A peerless Zauberkraft is needed
so we can hope to reach tomorrow, the day after tomorrow
trading like this and devoting oneself to managing—
without hurtling down into the nebulae
without slipping in a single false step, a seven-league one
Don't return to the decency of the mineral state
  Zauberkraft is my quarter
  the structure of the mind I don't feel possible
  the optical-mental illumination
  functions with uncertain schedules—it's confusing me
  But I guarantee, I sign promissory notes
  on Zauberkraft paths
  in small Zauberkraft rooms
  even without a tiny string phlebo tube;
  and through some tiny artery—see—the circle reactivates
  the registry office always gleams
How much   it cost you to stay on
managing up here in the quarter
and, for me already shoved and shouldered where it invades
there was such mania, quarter, to
support you, alone in all your starry

forza, inattualità, demoralizzazione costituzionale
e sovrumana inerzia di presenza
sempre più immagicata in colori linee piani—
forse a farli volare basterà un battito di mani.

strength, inactuality, constitutional demoralization
and superhuman inertia of presence
always more magicked in colors planes lines—
a handclap might be enough to make them fly.

Onde éli

Onde éla mai la pi cara de le mé jèje
che la scrivéa par carnevai e feste
i "dialoghi" in puisia e fin
co drento parole in latin
che tanti i se li recorda ancora;
"la se 'véa trat al béver," i diséa,
par passarghe sora a la malora.
Chi sa. Ma sol che éla la sa quant
che inte 'sto scribinciar mi ghe soméje.

Dove sono

Dove è mai la più cara delle mie zie
che scriveva per carnevali e feste
i dialoghi in poesia, perfino
con dentro parole in latino
che tanti li ricordano ancora;
"si era data al bere" dicevano,
per passar sopra alla malora.
Chi sa. Ma soltanto lei sa quanto
in questo scribacchiare le assomiglio.

Where Are They?

Where on earth is the dearest of my aunts
who used to write little plays
in verse for Carnival and other holidays
with Latin words thrown in to boot;
many people still remember them.
"She started drinking," they said,
to drown her sorrows.
Who knows. But only she knows
how much, in this scribbling, I resemble her.

Onde éla la Pina dei giornai
e la só botegheta drio la piazha
coi color che lustréa come ferai . . .
"Rivendita carbone e giornali":
negra pedo de 'n camin, co' i grun
de garbon, e in medo—che canpanele e sonai!—
al ros e 'l blu e 'l verdo dei giornai
al se destiréa e 'l cresséa
'fa 'n pradusel de mareveje—
ma 'l garbon ne rivéa fin su le zhéje.

Dov'è la Pina dei giornali
e la sua botteguccia dietro la piazza
coi colori brillanti come fanali . . .
"Rivendita carbone e giornali":
nera più di un camino, coi mucchi
di carbone, e in mezzo—che campanelle e sonagli!—
il rosso il blu e il verde dei giornali
si allargava e cresceva
come un praticello di meraviglie—
ma il carbone ci arrivava fino alle ciglia.

Where is Pina who sold newspapers
and her little shop behind the square
with colors bright as street lights . . .
"Coal and newspapers for sale":
blacker than a chimney, with piles
of coal all around, and in the middle—what bells! what rattles!—
the red blue green of the newspapers
spread and grew
like a marvellous meadow—
though the coal came up to our eyelashes.

Onde éla infra le amighe de me jèia
cussita bone tute e cussì stranbe
quela vedova Bres che vegnéa da Belun
e al loto la vinzhéa senpre i só anbi
e in pì la 'véa redità da só òn
otanta carte da mili, un balon
de schei, ma pò la 'véa magnà-su tut
a frajar, far savoia co 'ste amighe:
no l'era altro che sopete coade, graspin, govet,
onbrete e conpagnia bela,
anca si zherti no lo cret.

Dov'è tra le amiche di mia zia
così buone tutte e così strane
quella vedova Bres che veniva da Belluno
e al lotto vinceva sempre i suoi ambi
e in più aveva ereditato dal marito
ottantamila lire, una quanitità
di soldi, ma aveva poi scialacquato tutto
a spassarsela, a far baldoria con queste amiche:
non erano altro che zuppe covate (*piatto veneto*), grappini, uova,
bicchieri di vino e compagnia,
anche se certi non lo credono.

Where—among my aunt's friends,
all so good and so strange—
is the widow Bres, who came from Belluno
and always had winning lottery numbers
and had inherited a stack of money too
(eighty thousand lire) from her husband
but then frittered it all away
having fun, going on sprees with her friends:
nothing but hearty soups, grappa, eggs,
glasses of wine and all the rest,
even if certain people don't believe it.

Onde éla la Urora e i buzholà
e le caròbole e i sòrboi che la ghe vendéa
ai cèi par diese schei: che marcà
ala festa, drio vespro, che i ghe féa!
Su 'l fornelet sora 'l balcon podà
intant la só zheneta la bojéa:
ma i tosatan un dì drento inte 'l brodo
un zhochet de morer i ghe 'véa mes—
e ela col piron catando dur co la inpiréa—
"A che tenp, la diséa, che son tiradi ades."

Dov'è l'Aurora e i dolcini
e le carrube e i sorbi che vendeva
ai bimbi per dieci centesimi: che mercato
alla festa, dopo vespro, le facevano!
Sul fornelletto poggiato sul davanzale
intanto la sua cenetta bolliva:
ma i ragazzacci un giorno dentro il brodo
le avevano messo un piccolo ceppo di gelso—
e lei trovando duro quando tastava con la forchetta—
"A che tempi, diceva, oggi ci siamo ridotti!"

Where is Aurora and the cookies,
the dried carob beans, the crab apples that she sold
to children for a penny: what booming business
on holidays in the evenings the kids gave her!
On a camp stove, meanwhile, resting on the windowsill,
her supper would be boiling.
One time some big kids
put a small chunk of mulberry in her soup—
and when she tried it with her fork it seemed awfully hard—
"The world's going to hell in a handbasket," she used to say.

Onde éli Toni e la Neta
quei che in *Pasque* o dhà menzhonà
e mai che basta se menzhonarà
co la Catina só tosa e me vermana
a la lontana . . .
La era stata a Perosa Argentina
fora par al Piamont, a laorar,
inte 'na fabrica moderna e fina
e la ghen 'véa ben storie da contar:
nò de le diese ore sui teler
che sgràmola le teste col bacan
ma dele brave suore
del pensionato 'ndove che la 'stéa:
pensève, ogni matina cossa che le ghe déa:
cicolata calda, calda che la fuméa—
e noaltri, tosatei, a boca verta, co ela se la bevéa.

Dove sono Toni ed Annina
quelli che in *Pasque* ho già ricordati
e mai tanto che basta si dovranno ricordare
con Caterina loro figlia e mia cugina
alla lontana . . .
Era stata a Perosa Argentina
via per il Piemonte, a lavorare,
in una fabbrica moderna e raffinata
e aveva molte storie da raccontare:
non delle dieci ore sui telai
che sgranocchiano le teste col baccano,
ma delle brave suore
del pensionato dove lei abitava:
figuratevi ogni mattina cosa le davano:
cioccolata calda, calda che fumava—
e noi, bambini, a bocca aperta con lei la si beveva.

Where are Tony and Annina
whom I have already mentioned in *Pasque*
and who can never be remembered enough
with Caterina their daughter, my cousin
many times removed . . .
She had gone to Perosa Argentina
by way of Piedmont to work,
in a factory that was modern and sophisticated
and she had lots of stories to tell:
not about the ten-hour days hunched over the looms
that split your head with their racket
but about the kind nuns
who ran the boarding-house where she stayed:
quess what they gave her every morning:
hot chocolate, so hot the steam glistened—
and we kids, open-mouthed, drank it with her as we listened.

Onde éla la Marieta Tamòda
(femminile del cognome, anzi soprannome "Tamò")
spezialista del primo dei Dumas:
a memoria la contéa, parola par parola
tut quel che inte quei libri l'era capità.
La lavéa montagne de roba dó inte 'l Suligo,
da restar là incandìdi dal borin
o da assarghe la pel sbrissando sul jazhin,
ma la só testa l'era inte l'intrigo
de Faria, Montecristo, D'Artagnan,
dei moschetier saldi del re
che i féa fora zhaltron e zhacaran.
La domenega, chieta, in pince-nez
sentada vizhin a'n foghet de busie
o de istà sot le foie del morer,
la coréa, stajon par stajon, tuta la Franzha
desmentegandose 'l brontolar de la panzha
sóa e de só fioi—ela, drìoghe ai moschetier.
Nò, no ghe n'é sletran, abocato, né profeta
che àpie let scartafazhi pi de la Marieta!
. . . .

Dov'è Marietta Tamòda
(femminile del cognome, anzi soprannome "Tamò")
specialista del primo dei Dumas:
a memoria raccontava, parola per parola,
tutto ciò che in quei libri era avvenuto.
Lavava montagne di roba nel Soligo,
da restare canditi dal vento
o da lasciar la pelle scivolando sul ghiaccio,
ma la sua testa era nell'intrigo
di Faria, Montecristo, D'Artagnan,
dei moschettieri bravi del re
che facevano fuori cialtroni e ciarlatani.
La domenica, tranquilla, in pince-nez
seduta vicino a un focherello di trucioli
o in estate sotto le foglie del gelso,
correva, stagione a stagione, tutta la Francia
dimenticando il brontolare della pancia
sua e dei suoi figli—lei, dietro ai moschettieri.
No, non c'è letterato, avvocato, né profeta
che abbia letto scartafacci più della Marietta.
. . . .

Where is Marietta Tamòda
(with her feminine last name, her nickname "Tamò")
a first-rate Dumas specialist:
she could recite by heart word for word
everything that had happened in their books.
She washed mountains of stuff in the Soligo river,
leaving it there to be bleached by the wind
or she risked her neck by slipping on the ice,
but her head was spinning with the intrigues
of Faria, Montecristo, D'Artagnan,
the king's brave musketeers
who struck down charlatans and rogues.
On Sundays, serenely, with her pince-nez,
sitting by a little fire of wood shavings
or in summer under the leaves of the mulberry tree,
she would cross, season by season, the whole of France
forgetting her belly's grumbling
and that of her children, while following the musketeers.
No, there isn't a lawyer, prophet, or man of letters
who has read more adventure stories than Marietta!
. . . .

Aneme sante e bone
mi no so si ò fat mal
a tirarve 'fa calcamonìe
o fursi 'fa stris e scarpìe
sul parabris de l'auto
vecia che la se strassina
de not inte 'na sbóa,
    aneme sante e bone
    de la contrada e anca de pi in là
. . . .

        A, ma me par che 'l monte
        da 'n canton del cortivet
        un udor fondo scur e petadizh
        che 'l ciapa-dentro, 'l stornis
        inte le só vis'ciade
        ma caro caro—quel dei cavalier
        a mier sui só gardizh

Anime sante e buone
non so se ho fatto male
a ridurvi come decalcomanie
o forse come strisce e ragnatele
sul parabrezza dell'auto
vecchia che si trascina
di notte in una bufera
    anime sante e buone
    della contrada e anche di più in là
. . . .

        Ah, ma mi par che monti
        da un canto del cortiletto
        un odore fondo scuro e attaccaticcio
        che avvolge, stordisce
        nel suo vischio
        ma caro caro—quello dei bachi da seta
        a migliaia sui loro graticci

Good and kindly souls
I don't know if I've done wrong
by reducing you to decals
or maybe to streaks and spiderwebs
on the windshield of an old car
that drags along in the stormy night,
      good and saintly souls
      of the quarter and also beyond
. . . .

Ah, but a strange odor seems to be rising
from a corner of the courtyard,
an odor deep, dark, and sticky
that enfolds and dazes you
in its snare—
but precious beyond words—
it's the odor of silkworms
thousands of them on their trellises.

Gramolete che le fa na piovesina,
scheet che i casca inte la musina . . .
E ti, siben che tu te sent
fora del mazh, tu sé squasi content
e tu pensa a 'n bisset pi brut che bel
ma da la só seda infassà
lassù inte 'l terzho zhiel.[1]

Mandibolette che fanno una pioggerella,
soldi che cascano nel salvadanaio . . .
E tu, sebbene ti senta
fuori luogo, sei quasi contento
e pensi ad un insetto più brutto che bello
ma dalla sua seta fasciato
lassù nel terzo cielo.

Noi-io lumi di moccio, ci risolvemmo,
in finissimo etra
o magari in sciolina

Nella decalcomania
ogni riga è sfasata
e dovrebbe essere al posto di una precedente
Occorre un tenue conato di vomito
per riportarsi al punto giusto di lettura
            un dentello di rincorsa e poi
    scivolio lungo le giustezze
    volo di velleità: rècipe[2]
    rècipe rècipe: sciolina

Tiny jaws that dribble,
coins that fall into the money-box . . .
And you, although you feel out of place, are almost content
and you are thinking of an insect, more ugly than beautiful,
one wrapped, however, in its silk
up there in the seventh heaven.

We-I lights of slime, we were transformed,
into very fine ether
or maybe into wax

Under the decalcomania
every line is out of place
and should be in the place of the preceding one
A tenuous impulse to vomit is needed
to take one back to the right point in the reading
            run up in a jump and then
    a slide along the margins of the page
    a flight of fancy: recipe
    recipe recipe: wax

1. *T.N.*: The dialect section of the original poem ends here. The stanzas that follow are in Italian.

2. *T.N.*: *Recipe* is an archaic medical term synonomous with *prescription*. Here the archaic term is used to convey Zanzotto's desire to suggest an allusion to the kind of medical doctor found in Molière.

No te pias véder pióver sul bagnà
(ma ades scravazha), né che zhuite i porte
dó par Atene, o legne e roe 'nte 'l bòsch.
Par questo, asséi difizhil no basta che stranbo
me par mandarte, Eusebio, par casa versi—
co no fusse un de quei sonet tajadi justi come stèle,
che se uséa meter dó al ciaro de 'n mòcol,
co la gabana ados inte 'l fret dei gran tènp del passà.
Ris'ce cussì 'sta òlta de intrigarme
e de inverigolarme pèdo che par al solito;
quant mèjo un taser fondo, taser e lèderte.
    Ma par quei sbari de s'ciòp o de mine
    inte 'l pi raro vodo dei canp, dei mondi,
    e pi ancora par quei racolar de rochéte
    sufiade su in s'ciantis de sagra
    e in sghirli de ventade fin dentro le nèole,—
    che senpre i sbocia da la tó poesia,—
    che senpre i me desmissia
    e che tanti ani fa me 'véa segnà 'na strada
    cofà tra mèdo de 'na calivèra,—
    bisogna pur che te salude, ancó.
    No so si drét son 'ndat, si ò scantiná,

Non ti piace veder piovere sul bagnato
(ma ora diluvia), né che portino civette
giù ad Atene, o legna e rovi al bosco.
Per questo, assai difficile oltre che bizzarro
mi sembra, Eusebio, mandarti versi in casa—
non fosse uno di quei sonetti tagliati giusti come schegge di legno
  da ardere,
che si usava stendere a lume di candela,
con un tabarro indosso nel freddo dei grandi tempi del passato.
Rischio così questa volta di impacciarmi
e di succhiellarmi peggio che di solito;
quanto migliore un tacere profondo, tacere e leggerti.
    Ma per quegli spari di fucile o (scoppi) di mine
    nel più raro vuoto delle campagne, dei mondi,
    e più ancora per quel raganellare di mortaretti
    soffiati sù in lampi di sagra
    e in vortici di vento fin dentro le nubi (tempestose)—
    che sempre sbocciano-sboccano dalla tua poesia,—
    che sempre mi risvegliano
    e che tanti anni addietro mi avevano segnato una strada
    come nel mezzo di un banco di nebbie—
    bisogna pure che oggi io ti saluti.
    Non so se sono andato dritto o se ho deviato,

For Eugenio Montale on His Eightieth Birthday

You don't like to see coals carried to Newcastle,
(although that's what I'm doing)
owls brought to Athens or firewood and brambles to the forest.
That's why it seems so difficult, and bizarre too,
to send you a poem, Eusebius—
unless it were one of those sonnets cut, like chips of kindling, just right,
like the ones they used to draft by candlelight
bundled up in a heavy cloak against the cold in the great days gone by.
This time I risk making a mess of things
and I'm mixed up worse than usual;
how much better a deep silence, keeping quiet and reading your poems.
    And yet, because of those rifle shots,
    those mine explosions in the rarest void
    of the countrysides, of the worlds,
    and even more for that crackle of squibs
    blown upward in festival flashes
    in the vortices of wind
    in the very heart of storm clouds,—
    that always bud and bloom from your poetry,—
    and always rouse me
    and which, many years ago, showed me a road
    as in the middle of a fog bank—
    that's why I must greet you today.
    I don't know if I have gone straight or if I have deviated,

si de farse capir 'ste righe merite
che da zhope e da rive lontane te mande.
Ma son siguro che ti tu vét quant lanpido
l'é l'agurar che mi—co tanti altri—te fae
par i tó otanta de 'sta umana vita
e fursi mili de sgorlarne-incantarne
col tó scur col tó lustro
col tó serarte in rizh e col tó pànderte:
ran e radis de l'istessa boscaja
onde che fazhil, difizhil, tra lori ingatiadi,
i é senpre lori e senpre 'l só contrari.

se meritino di farsi capire queste righe
che da balze e declivi lontani ti mando.
Ma sono certo che tu vedi quanto limpido
è l'augurio che io—con tanti altri— ti faccio
per i tuoi ottanta di questa umana vita
e forse mille di scrollarci-incantarci
col tuo buio col tuo luccicare
col tuo chiuderti a riccio e col tuo renderti manifesto:
rami e radici della stessa selva
dove facile e difficile, tra loro aggrovigliati,
sono sempre se stessi e sempre il loro contrario.

if these lines, sent from distant cliffs and slopes,
merit understanding.
But I'm sure that you see how clear
is the wish that I (along with many others)
make for your eighty years of this human life,
and perhaps a thousand more as well of your jolting-entrancing us
with your darkness, your sparkle,
your hedgehog obscurity and self-disclosure:
branches and roots of the same forest
where the easy and the difficult tangled up together
are always themselves and always their opposites.

In ricordo de Pasolini

Ti tu magnéa la tó ciòpa de pan
sul treno par andar a scola
tra Sazhil e Conejan;
mi ere póch lontan, ma a quei tènp là
diese chilometri i era 'na imensità.
Cussita é stat che 'lora
do tosatèi no i se à mai cognossést.
Ma quande mai se 'varàelo podést
catarse sote 'l stesso pòrtego
de 'na stazhioneta in medo ai canp
co 'l só canpanelet che 'l fa ten ten ten ten
disèndone quant fondo che é 'l seren—
    e intant ore dornade e stajon
    le va via co l'onbrìa che la scrif,
    par case e vieri par muret e pra
    par bus zhiése e canton,
    radis e scarabizh?
Ma quande mai, prima che 'l treno l' rive,
se 'varàelo fat ora
par quele do tre ciàcole,
le sole che pól dar sora 'sta tera
de cognosserne 'n póch, póch ma devera?

In ricordo di Pasolini

Tu mangiavi il tuo pane
sul treno per andare a scuola
tra Sacile e Conegliano;
io ero poco lontano, ma a quei tempi
dieci chilometri erano un'immensità.
Così avvenne che allora
due ragazzetti non si sono conosciuti.
Ma quando mai avremmo potuto
trovarci sotto la stessa pensilina
di una stazioncina in mezzo ai campi
col suo campanello che fa ten ten ten ten
dicendoci quanto profondo è il sereno—
    e intanto ore giornate e stagioni
    se ne vanno con l'ombra che scrive,
    per case e vetri muriccioli e prati
    per siepi e dovunque per luoghi reconditi,
    radici e segni illeggibili?
Ma quando mai prima che il treno arrivi,
avremmo fatto a tempo
per quel po' di chiacchiericcio,
il solo che può dare su questa terra
che ci si conosca un poco, poco ma davvero?

In Memory of Pasolini

You used to eat your bread on the way to school
riding the train
between Sacile and Conegliano;
I lived close by, but in those days
ten kilometers was a huge distance.
And so it happened that at the time
two boys didn't get to know each other.
But when could we have met
under the same roof
of a little station in the middle of fields
with its bell going ding ding ding ding
telling us how deep the clear sky is—
    and meanwhile hours days and seasons
    vanish with the shadow that through windows,
    through houses, low walls, meadows,
    through hedges, and everywhere in hidden places,
    writes roots and illegible signs?
But when, ever, before the train pulled in,
would we have found time,
for that bit of chatter,
the only thing you can exchange on this earth,
so that you get to know another person slightly, slightly but truly?

Se se à parlà, pi avanti, se se à ledést;
zherte òlte 'von tasést o se à sticà,
la vita ne à parà sote straségne
e ciapà-dentro par tamài diversi,
mi fermo, inpetolà 'nte i versi,
ti dapartut co la tó passion de tut;
ma pur ghe n'era 'n fil che 'l ne tegnéa:
de quel che val se 'véa l'istessa idea.

Mi te spetèe qua sù, 'ndove che ancora
coi só lustrin i suspira i alba pratalia
ma senpre pi marzhi de sote e parsora;
ti tu sé restà là col tó corajo,
'ndove che pi la zhavària l'Italia.

Ah, scùseme, se ades no so darte
altro che 'sto muzhigamènt, 'ramai da vecio . . .
L'é sol che 'n pore sforzh, tremor,
par pontar-sù, justar-sù in qualche modo
—par un momento sol, par saludarte—
quel che i à fat dei tó os e del tó cor.

Più avanti, ci siamo parlati, ci siamo letti;
certe volte abbiamo taciuto o abbiamo litigato,
la vita ci ha spinti sotto sgocciolamenti di acqua fredda (colpi)
e presi in trappole diverse,
io fermo, impiastricciato nei versi,
tu dappertutto con la tua passione di tutto;
ma pur c'era un filo che sempre ci legava:
di ciò che vale avevamo la stessa idea.

Io ti aspettavo quassù, dove ancora
coi loro scintillii sospirano gli alba pratalia (distese bianche di neve)
ma sempre più guasti al di sotto e al di sopra;
tu sei rimasto là col tuo coraggio,
dove più delira l'Italia.

Ah, scusami se ora non so darti
altro che questo borbottio, da vecchio ormai . . .
È solo un povero sforzo, tremore,
per ricucire, riconnettere in qualche modo
—per un momento solo, per salutarti—
quello che hanno fatto delle tue ossa e del tuo cuore.

Later we talked, we read each other's work;
sometimes we kept silent or we argued,
life pushed us under drippings of cold water (blows)
and caught us in different traps,
me, motionless, mired in poetry,
you, everywhere, with your passion for everything;
but there was always a thread that linked us:
we had the same idea of what really matters.

I was waiting for you up here, where the dawn meadows
(white expanses of snow) still sigh with their sparkling
but always more spoiled above and down below;
you, with your courage, remained fixed,
where Italy is most delirious.

Ah forgive me if all I can give you now
is this old man's mumbling . . .
It's only a tremor, a poor effort
to stitch together again, patch up somehow
—for just a moment, to say farewell—
what they did with your bones and with your heart.

Co l'é mort la Toti

L'era 'n dì de jenaro, de solesel,
no paréa gnanca fret—tu era ti
che tu taséa par mai pi
ma co n' tàser lidier 'fa rosada
    che se inbròsa inte 'l fondi de la strada
    'ndove che tut se fa blu

E l' paréa 'n funeralet
fat da 'n pochi de cèi,
no ghe n'era pi né bei né bruti
e i siori no era pi siori
e i poreti, gnanca pi lori,
parché santi e tosatèi se era tuti
co na s'cióna lustra atorno i cavei—
    tuti ingrumadi col nostro pesar
    atorno de la tó cassa
    squasi par no assarte 'ndar

E l' sindico, bulo, cola só fassa,
l'à mes-su in mèdo ai fior
sul fonografo 'n disco dei tói
"Un bel dì vedremo"
e le era bandiere, panesèi, nastri de color
inte 'n ciaro de vènt sora i pra

Quando morì la Toti

Era un giorno di gennaio, di solicello,
non sembrava nemmeno freddo—eri tu
che tacevi per mai più
ma con un silenzio lieve qual rugiada
    che si fa brina sul fondo della strada
    ove tutto diviene blu

E sembrava un funeralino
fatto da alcuni bambini
e non c'eran più belli né brutti
e i signori non eran signori
e i poveri, non eran più loro,
perché santi e fanciulli si era tutti
con un anello lucente intorno ai capelli—
    tutti ammucchiati col nostro pesare
    intorno alla tua cassa
    quasi per non lasciarti andare

E il sindaco, fiero, con la sua fascia
posò in mezzo ai fiori
sul grammofono un disco dei tuoi
"Un bel dì vedremo"
ed eran bandiere, pannolini, nastri di colori
in un chiarore di vento sui prati

When Toti Died

It was a sunny day in January,
it hardly seemed cold—you were the one
silenced forevermore
but with a stillness light as dew
    changing to frost at the end of the street
    where everything turns blue

It seemed a play funeral
put on by children,
no one was beautiful or ugly
the rich were no longer rich
and the poor were no longer themselves,
because everybody had become saint or child
with a shining ring round their hair—
    all heaped with our weight
    around your casket
    as though not to let you go

And the mayor, gallant in his sash,
put a record of your
"Un bel dì vedremo"
on the phonograph among the flowers
and there were flags, scraps of cloth, colored ribbons
in a brightness of wind over the meadows

inte 'n ciaro de dì ben destinà.
E ognun, anca chi che piandéa,
l'era ciapà-dentro, stornì
'fa da 'n dolzh de rosada
da 'n dolzh de dolor
a sentir a sentir
    quel che restéa de ti
prometer senzha ma, senzha chissà
a tuti 'n s'ciant, 'na ala,
un grìsol che no fala:
"No, gnessun no pól morir
    no l' morirà."

in un chiarore di giorno ben destinato.
E ognuno, anche chi piangeva
era preso, stordito
come da una dolcezza di rugiada
da una dolcezza di dolore
a sentire a sentire
    ciò che di te restava
promettere senza "ma," senza "chissà"
a tutti una scheggia, un'ala,
un brivido che non falla:
"No, nessuno può morire
    nessuno morirà."

in the brightness of a day clearly marked by destiny.
And everyone, even those who were weeping,
was bewildered, struck dumb,
as if by a softness of dew
by a sweetness of sorrow
listening and listening hard
        to what was left of you
promising with no "buts," no "who knows"
to one and all a splinter, a wing,
a shiver unfailing:
"No, nobody can die
        nobody will ever die."

Sarlòt e Jijeto

E cussì tu sé 'ndat anca ti, Sarlòt,
dhà che gnessun resta qua par semenzha,
ma tu sé 'ndat come che l'era justa
come che capita par la Sunta o la Sensa—
Cossa de pi bel che stusarse
cussita vecio che tu sé tornà tosatel
anzhi ancora pi indrio,
par mocàrtela quacio
inte 'n bòcol lidiero, la not de Nadal.
Se 'véa bisoin che qualchidun
al ne dèsse la proa
che ghe n'é, che i se fa dì par dì, che i nas i dii;
l'era tant che no se vedéa
de 'ste céte, insonegade mareveje
come 'l tàser polsà
de 'sta not, che 'l gran fret se à smolà,
e le nodéa le stele
inte 'n prà squasi tèpido,
come che rare òlte l'é a Nadal—
e ghe n'é quel sprumor
che se sènt e no se sènt:
l'é l' sol
che sote le cuerte de lopa e de scur,
picinin, delicato, 'l se insonia de l'istà.

Charlot e Gigetto

E così te ne sei andato anche tu, Charlot,
poiché nessuno resta qui per semenza,
ma sei andato nel modo più giusto
come avviene per l'Assunzione e l'Ascensione—
Che di più bello che spegnersi
così vecchio che sei tornato bambino
anzi ancora più indietro,
per svignartela quatto
in una bolla leggera, la notte di Natale.
Avevamo bisogno che qualcuno
ci desse la prova
che ci sono, si fanno giorno per giorno, nascono gli dei;
da tanto non si vedevano
di queste quiete, insonnolite meraviglie
come il tacere riposato
di questa notte, che il gran freddo si è fiaccato
e nuotavano le stelle
in un prato quasi tiepido,
come di rado avviene a Natale—
e c'è un effluvio
che si sente e non si sente:
è il sole
che sotto le coperte di muschio e d'oscuro,
piccolo, delicato, sta sognando l'estate.

Charlie Chaplin and Gigetto

And so you too are gone, Charlie,
since nobody lives forever
but you've left in the best way
just like the Assumption or the Ascension—
What's more beautiful than to expire?
so old you become a child again,
no, even younger,
slipping off on the sly
in a light bubble Christmas night.
We needed somebody
to give us proof
that they exist, that day by day they're made, the gods are born;
For so long they hadn't been seen
these quiet unsleeping marvels
like the restful stillness
of this night that's broken the bitter cold,
and the stars were swimming
in a meadow that's almost warm,
as rarely happens at Christmas time—
and there's a vapor
that's felt and not felt:
it's the sun that,
under blankets of moss and darkness
small, delicate, dreams of summer.

Ghe voléa pur che 'na òlta qualchidun
al sbrissolèsse via
co la stessa braura che le à le comete
ma anca quel penacét de fun
che 'l vien da sora i grun de stran brusà,
ma anca quel rujet de aqua medo jazhà,
che, se 'n poch i lo scolta,
l'à ancora da far do ciàcole
co la stessa furbaria tóa, Sarlòt.
Se mai un l'é scanpà
da le onge dei orchi tu sé ti 'nte 'sta not,
col tó pas inbraghessà,
in scapinèle o co i tó do scarpon,
che 'l te portarà senzha fadiga
fòra de ogni cadena, de ogni triga
'ndove che brazh de galassie e calcamoníe de misteri
i é pronti a far jonda par ti, pore òn, pore sovran
o dèo fresch, apena batidà.

Ma l'é 'na finta, 'l so mi, anca questa qua:
ti no tu 'ndarà massa lontan,
tu starà qua drio de 'n muret
o de 'na zhiesa a far ba-bau
co la tó capelina e la tó bagolina

Bisognava pure che una volta qualcuno
scivolasse via
con la stessa bravura che hanno le comete,
ma anche quel pennacchietto di fumo
che vien da sopra i mucchi di strame bruciato,
ma anche quel rivolo d'acqua mezzo gelato
che, se un poco l'ascoltano,
ha due chiacchiere ancora da fare
con la tua stessa furberia, Charlot.
Se mai uno è sfuggito
dalle unghie degli orchi sei tu in questa notte,
col tuo passo goffo nei pantaloni
in calzini o coi tuoi due scarponi,
che ti porteranno senza fatica
fuori d'ogni catena, d'ogni imbroglio
dove bracci di galassie e decalcomanie di misteri
son pronti a farti gran festa, pover'uomo, povero sovrano
o dio di fresco, appena battezzato.

Ma è una finta, anche questa, io lo so:
tu non andrai troppo lontano,
sarai qui dietro un muretto
o dietro una siepe a far "bau,"
con il tuo cappelluccio ed il tuo bastoncino

We really needed somebody for once
to slip away
with the same bravura that the comets have
but also with the tiny feather of smoke
that comes from over heaps of burned straw,
but also with the trickle of half-frozen water,
that, if listened to a little,
still has some chattering to do
with your same slyness, Charlie.
        If anyone's ever escaped
from the ogres' clutches, it's you this night,
with your clumsy walk in baggy pants
wearing socks or your two big shoes
that will carry you without effort
beyond every chain, every difficulty,
where the arms of galaxies and the decalcomanias of mysteries
stand waiting to throw a big party for you, poor man, poor sovereign
or new, just baptized god.

But, this is a trick too, I know:
you won't go very far away,
you'll be here behind a wall
or behind a bush ready to shout "boo"
with your little hat and cane

e i tó òci che òcia e i tó mostaci,
par farghe a qualchidun la ganbarola,
par slongarghe 'na scòpola scondendo la man;
parché tu à da far—se l'ocor, —anca 'l Barbablù
cofà monsieur Verdoux,
par inpirar de colpo
chi che vol farte massa caramel,
parché tu sarà senpre 'n bisnènt un sacrament
par recordarne slama e piera
fin che ghen sarà chi che patis la fan
e chi che se fa guera.

O cussì ben partì
o cussì ben rivà da restar anca qua,
assa che insieme co ti
me pense de Jijeto
che l'é stat al Sarlòt del me paese
inte quel tenp che oramai
lunari no l' ghe n'à pi.
Parché ghe n'era inte ogni paese un tó fradel
che 'l voléa somejarte e copiarte
e che co la só arte
bonazha e parché 'l restéa senpre 'n porecan
al portéa 'l mèjo de ti dapartut.

e i tuoi occhi che adocchiano e i tuoi baffi
per fare a qualcuno lo sgambetto,
per allungargli uno schiaffo nascondendo la mano;
perché devi fare, se occorre, anche il Barbablù
come Monsieur Verdoux,
fino a infilzare d'un tratto
chi vuol farti troppo caramello
perché sarai sempre un misero e un tipaccio
per ricordarci fango e pietra
fin che ci sarà chi patisce la fame
e chi si fa la guerra.

O così ben partito
o così ben arrivato da rimanere anche qui,
lascia che insieme con te
io ricordi anche Gigetto
che è stato lo Charlot del mio paese
in quel tempo che ormai
non ha più calendari.
Perché c'era in ogni paese un tuo fratello
che voleva somigliarti e copiarti
e che con la sua arte
bonaria e perché sempre restava un poveraccio
portava il meglio di te dappertutto.

and your eyes giving the once over and your moustache,
waiting to trip somebody up,
to give them a slap hiding your hand;
because you've got to be prepared, if need be, to become Bluebeard,
like Monsieur Verdoux
ready to run through suddenly
anyone who wants to take advantage of you,
because you'll always be poor and a character
to remind us of mud and stone
as long as there are people suffering from hunger,
and those who make war.

Oh so well departed
oh so well arrived so that you remain here too,
let me, along with you,
recall Gigetto
who was the Charlie of my town
in those days that by now
no calendar records.
Because every town had one of your brothers
who wanted to be like you and copy you
and your good-natured art
and because he always stayed poor
he took the best of you everywhere.

A Jijéto inte 'l scur daghe na man
e ménelo co ti de foravia:
l'é bon anca de farte
—l'é 'l so' mistier—una fotografia (in Kirlian).
Ma òcio, che l'é furbo anca lu,
che 'na lugànega o 'na palanca o 'na stèla
par scaldarse lassù inte i bus del blu,
o 'n fulminante par inpizharghe bubarate
no 'l te fae sparir dala scarsèla
par tegnerseli lu
o magari tornàrteli, co 'n pie 'nte'l cul.

Sarlòt, mena Jijeto
mena tuti i Jijeti del passà
che i voléa far na cubia co ti
a trasformar inte 'na gran ridada
tut al gran viajo co le só stazhion—
inte la mejo farsa
che se àpie mai vist in cosmorama,
anca si l'é tuta piena
de straségne e sgrifon:
programa:
"Sarlòt che sfida a diesemili dóghi
e fa fessa la mort in tuti i lóghi,

A Gigetto nell'oscurità dà una mano
e portalo con te alla chetichella:
è anche capace di farti
—è il suo mestiere—una fotografia (in Kirlian).
Ma attento, che è furbo anche lui,
che una salsiccia o una monetina o una scheggia di legno
per scaldarsi lassù nei buchi del blu,
o un fiammifero per accendervi falò
non ti faccia
sparire dalla tasca per tenerseli lui
o magari ridarteli, con una pedata nel sedere.

Charlot, conduci Gigetto,
porta tutti i Gigetti del passato
che volevano far coppia con te
a trasformare in una gran risata
il gran viaggio con le sue stazioni—
nella più bella farsa
che sia mai stata vista in cosmorama,
anche se è tutta piena
di strisce e graffi:
programma:
"Charlot che sfida a diecimila giochi
e fa fessa la morte in ogni luogo,

Give a hand to Gigetto in the darkness
and secretly take him with you:
he can also make for you
—it's his job—a photograph (in Kirlian).
But watch out! he's crafty too,
don't let him snatch from your pocket
a sausage or a coin or a chip of wood
to warm himself up there in the holes of blue,
or a match to light bonfires,
to keep for himself
or give it back, with a swift kick in the rear end.

Charlie, take Gigetto
take all the Gigettos of the past
who wanted to be your partner
to transform into a big laugh
the great journey with all its stations—
into the most beautiful farce
ever seen in the cosmorama,
even if it's all full
of streaks and scratches.
Program:
"Charlie challenges Death to ten thousand games
and beats his ass everywhere,

qua dó, lassù 'nte 'l giro imenso del Nadal"
co lu, Jijeto e noaltri
e tuti i altri inte 'l só cast.

NOTA

Dopo 'n pochi de dì, do Sarlòt
de adès, anzhi nò, do cius, do gnoch,
a cavar su 'l tó zhendre i à proà
e pò inte 'l zhendre, par gnent, i à frazhà
e pò i à assà tut quant in medo a 'n prà
e pò, 'fa tì, i se à catà in preson; pazhienzha:
ma l'é cussì che devera
la seguita a durar la to semenzha.
(Mah, sto afar qua
me par che squasi tu l'àpie parecià
ti, e par testament assà da rezhitar . . .)

quaggiù, lassù nel giro immenso del Natale"
con lui, Gigetto e noi
e tutti nel suo cast.

Nota

Dopo alcuni giorni due Charlot
di oggi, anzi no, due tonti, due balordi,
a trar su le tue ceneri hanno provato,
e poi nelle ceneri, invano, hanno frugato
e poi tutto han lasciato in mezzo a un prato
poi, come te, si son trovati in prigione; pazienza:
ma è così che davvero,
sèguita a durare la tua semenza.
(Mah, questa storia
mi sembra quasi che l'abbia preparata
tu, e per testamento da recitare lasciata . . .)

down here, up there in the immense circle of Christmas"
with him, Gigetto and us
and everybody in his cast.

Note

After a few days, two present-day Charlies
no, two knuckleheads, two jerks I mean,
tried to dig up your ashes
and poked around in your ashes, in vain,
then left everything in the middle of a meadow
and then, like you, landed in jail; oh well:
but in this way
your seed really does live on.
(Wait a minute . . . this whole story
seems as though it's been rigged up by you
as a last will and testament to be read after your death . . .)

E S'CIAO

Checo, tant ben tu à parlà
'fa 'n mus pavan, contando robe trevisane,
e cussì ben tu a remenà color e tere
che no se savaràe pi dir, debòta,
da 'ndove che tu fusse. Ah sì che se podéa
'lora co ti, col bosch, mover làveri e lengua
e anca dendive e menton
e assarse andar tuti in fumane
e perder paese e nazhion
par deventar sol che un lodar, content
del só esser par calcossa e nò par gnent.
    Ma ades l'é 'n tòch che al bosch
via i ghe à sapà
tut quel só gran sermon
che ti tu 'véa scoltà
e tu ne 'véa portà, da bon spion;
ran, zhoch, s'césene, stran
a starnirne, a inbalsemarne fior,
osèi, fonghi, pavéi, bis, fuin, sprumor
de Ben e Mal che i se remissia intra de lori,
e i se muda un co l'altro, ciavandose, si i pol.
L'é justa, donca, che mi capisse poch al tó pavan
(e ti gnent, fursi, del mé pievesan)
par la reson che póch e gnent, 'romai,

E AMEN

Cecco, tanto bene hai parlato
come una mutria padovana, raccontando cose trevigiane,
e così bene hai mescolato colori e terre
che quasi non saprei più dire
di dove tu fossi. Ah certo si poteva
allor con te, col bosco, muovere labbra e lingua
e anche gengive e mento
e lasciarsi andare tutti in vampe d'entusiasmo
e perdere paese e nazionalità
per divenire soltanto un lodare, contento
del suo essere per qualcosa e non per nulla.
    Ma ora è un pezzo che al bosco
hanno zappato via
tutto quel suo gran sermone
che tu avevi ascoltato
e ci avevi portato, da buona spia;
rami, ceppi, schegge, strame
per farci la lettiera, fiori a darci il loro balsamo,
uccelli, funghi, farfalle, serpi, faine, intenso effluvio
di Bene e Male che si intricano tra loro,
e si mutano uno nell'altro, fregandosi, se possono.
È giusto, dunque, che poco io capisca il tuo pavano
(e tu niente, forse, del mio pievese)
per la ragione che quasi nulla ormai

AND AMEN

Cecco, you spoke so well
like a Paduan sourpuss, telling Trevisan tales,
and you mixed colors and soil so well
that I would be hard put to say any more
where you came from. Ah, certainly, one could,
in those days, move lips and tongue
and even gums and chin with you, with the woods,
and let everybody go off in flashes of enthusiasm,
lose country and nationality
to become only praise, content
with standing for something, not for nothing.
        But now, it's been quite some time,
since they hacked away
from the woods all of its grand preachings
that you listened to
and brought to us, like a good spy;
branches, stumps, splinters, litter
to provide bedding for us, flowers to give us their balm,
birds, mushrooms, butterflies, snakes, pole-cats, intense effluvium
of Good and Evil that get entangled with each other
and, rubbing together, change one into the other, if they can.
It's right, then, that I understand little of your Paduan tongue
(and you, perhaps, nothing at all of my Pieve dialect)
because almost nothing any more

da le to bande o fora par de qua,
al ghe someja 'n s'ciant a quel che tu à cantà.
E tant, pò, tant de pi del bosch
co lu é 'ndat pers, strazhà, sacagnà,
che tóo de ti, l'era, e 'nca méo de mi:
parché quel bosch che pur l'era salvàrego
al 'véa calcossa de anca massa mèstego,
al 'vea calcossa che lo féa de casa,
che féa tuti i só lóf e bólp e anguane,
struzhet e panigasse, zhisile cuch poiane,
figurete de 'n dógo, dissegnet
de 'n tosatel, o si se vól de 'n mistro,
ma che da senpre le ne era indentro indentro,
e da là le vegnéa pa' i nostri insonii
e sufiar, subiolar,
a gratolar drio de sfése e portele,
a fruzhar, furigar, far gatarìgole
intra coltrine e onbrìe
intra striche de sol inpolverì
inte 'l scur dei biaver
(bau-sète, nati-nati, bissi-bissi).
Sì, sì, tut quel che no savon de 'ver
o 'von desmentegà ma che l'é nostro
e de tuta la fola senzha fin che la é co noi,

dalle tue parti ed anche qui da noi,
somiglia un poco a ciò che tu hai cantato.
E tanto, tanto più del bosco
con lui si è perso, dissipato, acciaccato
che era tua proprietà, come anche mia:
perché quel bosco che pure era ispidamente intrattabile
aveva qualcosa di fin troppo mansueto,
aveva qualcosa che lo faceva di casa,
che rendeva tutti i suoi lupi e volpi e anguane,
sgriccioli e passeri, rondini cuculi e poiane,
figurine di un gioco, disegnini
di un bambino, o se si vuole di un maestro d'arte,
ma che da sempre ci eran dentro dentro,
e di là venivano attraverso i nostri sogni
a soffiare, fischiettare,
a sgranocchiare dietro fessure e porticine,
a tocchignare, a rovistare, a far solletico
fra tendine e ombre
fra strisce di sole vive di polvere
nel buio dei granai
(bau-sète, nati-nati, bissi-bissi).
E sì, sì, tutto quello che non sappiamo di avere
o abbiamo dimenticato ma che è nostro
e di tutta la folla senza fine che è con noi,

from your parts of the country and here in ours
resembles in the least what you sang about.
    And so much more of the woods
that were your property, as well as mine,
has been lost with it, laid waste, wrecked:
because those woods, harshly forbidding,
had contained something all too mild,
something that made it like a home,
made all of its wolves, foxes, and nymphs-witches-fairies,
wrens and sparrows, swallows, cuckoos and buzzards,
figures in a game, little drawings
done by a child, or if you will, a great master,
but that were always inside us, *deep* within,
and from there they would come by way of our dreams
to blow, hiss,
nibble, behind cracks and little doors,
to grope, rummage, tickle,
among curtains and shadows
among sun-streaks alive with dust
in the darkness of granaries
(hide-and-seek, peek-a-boo, I-spy).
    And yes, yes, everything we don't know we have
or have forgotten, but which is ours
and belongs to the whole endless throng that is with us,

Checo, no l'é mai stat cussita ben logà
né mejo savajà che inte 'l tó bosch, inte i tó sfoj.
(O bosch: cuiéra, casseleta,
cussin spuncià da 'n rabiosézh de aghét,
sachet da 'ndar a carità
pien de sòfego e arieta,
cavèi, stivele, remandèi,
tirache, ràcole, dàlmede, capèi
incrostoladi de jazh, recin,
sangue inpetrì col só dentin:
"I putèi del Mulineto
i va via co le ghete
e só mare va a strazzete
co la mussa e col caret . . .").
Tuti i só arte, i só dret,
tut quel che ne ocoréa par trarse fora
da le pétole, fusse qua a 'sto mondo
fusse anca par de là,
Checo, drento al tó bosch ti tu l'avea intanà.
E i tó momò magnéoi e s'cèti
i 'vea fat tut un buligar de lustro
su tut, come tochet de speci che i fa 'l diaolin;
da lontan un destin al prometéa

Cecco, non è mai stato sì ben collocato
né meglio sistemato che nel tuo bosco, nei tuoi fogli.
(O bosco: aiola d'orto, cassettina,
cuscino trapunto da un'irritazione di aghetti,
sacca per andare ad elemosina
piena d'afa e di fresco,
capelli, stivalucci, grimaldelli,
bretelle, raganelle di legno, zoccoli, cappelli
incrostati di ghiaccio, orecchini,
sangue coagulato col suo dentino:
"I bambini del Molinetto
vanno in giro con le ghette
e la lor mamma va a stracci
con l'asina e il carretto . . .").
Tutti gli arnesi, tutto ciò che fa comodo,
tutto quello che ci occorreva per trarci fuori
dai pasticci, fosse a questo mondo
foss'anche nell'aldilà,
Cecco, dentro il tuo bosco tu l'avevi intanato.
E le tue chiacchiere bonarie e schiette
avevano creato tutto un brulichio di luci
su tutto, come pezzi di specchio che vengono mossi per abbagliare;
di lontano un destino prometteva

Cecco, has never been as well arranged
or better organized than in your woods, in your pages.
(Oh woods: garden flower-bed, little chest,
cushion embroidered by an irritation of small needles,
beggar's sack
full of mustiness and fresh air,
hair, boots, jimmies,
suspenders, wooden clappers, clogs,
ice-encrusted hats, earrings,
clotted blood with its small tooth:
"The children of the Molinetto
go round with spats on
and their mamas go round in rags
with their donkey and their carts . . ."). 
All the tools, everything useful,
everything we needed to get out of trouble,
whether in this world,
or the next,
Cecco, you had holed up with you in your woods.
And your goodnatured, open chatter
had created a whole swarm of lights
on everything, like pieces of a mirror moved to dazzle;
from far off, a destiny was promising

senzha bale, 'l zhignéa 'fa 'n bon sensèr:
si no 'vè bu, sì in pò che 'vè da 'ver.

I à pestà-su, squacià-do, brusà
co manère e segat
pò co mine e canon
pò co ramade, restèi, capiòt, bandon
(pèdo de 'na queimada brasilèira):
epur al nostro bosch no 'l la met-dó.
Rumegando quei spin e pai-de-fer
e de cimento al cres de sora e par de fora,
Checo, de quel che ti tu à scrit, drìoghe a Magagnò,
pi in là de quel che mi l'ano passà
o olsà scriver, podandome
su un fiorun de os, su 'n scalin stort,
e fin su la tó testa-da-mort.
E te dae grazhie de no 'vérme refudà
al tó sal, le tó erbete fine da conzhar,
co se inbarbotéa o se ingrintéa 'l me straparlar:
tu sa che l'é 'fa quel che inte i confessonari
se ghe mola inte 'l vódo
inte 'l són de la recia a le teste-da-mort,
che no 'l pól esser de gnessun'antra sort.
E 'l nostro bosch a Mantel, strafantà

senza bugie, come un buon sensale ammiccava:
se non avete avuto, certo sì che dovrete avere.

Hanno spaccato, abbattuto, bruciato
con mannaie e gran seghe
poi con mine e cannoni
poi con reti metalliche, cancelli, casacce, tramezzi di lamiera
(peggio che una queimada brasileira):
eppure il nostro bosco non la smette.
Ruminando quelle spine e quelle spranghe di ferro
e di cemento, cresce di sopra e al di fuori,
Cecco, di ciò che hai scritto, seguendo Magagnò,
più in là di quel che l'anno scorso
ho osato scrivere, appoggiandomi
su un frammentìo d'ossa, su uno scalino storto
e anche sul tuo teschio.
E ti rendo grazie di non avermi rifiutato
il tuo sale, le tue fini erbette per condire,
quando si imbrogliava e si infuriava il mio parlare folle:
tu sai che esso è come quello che nei confessionali
si lascia andare nel vuoto
dell'osso temporale dei teschi,
e che non può essere di alcuna altra specie.
E il nostro bosco del Montello, strambamente sconvolto

without lies, winking like a good middleman:
if you haven't made it yet, you surely will.

They have split, chopped down, burned
with axes and huge saws,
then with mines and cannons
and afterwards with metal fences, gates, ugly houses, wire mesh partitions
(worse than a Brazilian *queimada*):
and yet our forest doesn't surrender.
Chewing on those thorns and those iron
and cement bars, it grows over and beyond them,
Cecco, from what you have written, following Magagnò,
further than I dared to write last year,
while leaning on a fragment of bone,
a warped step,
and also on your skull.
And I thank you for not having refused me
your salt, your fine herbs for seasoning,
when we got embroiled and my mad speech went wild:
you know that it's like the talk in the confessionals
when we let ourselves go into the void
of the frontal bone of skulls,
and that can't be of any other kind.
And our Montello woods, madly overthrown

ades e descunì
e trist come che 'l par,
assonlo star, fidonse
de lu—e de chi che vegnarà
(no élo cussì che 'na canta va fenida?),
asson che 'l ne asse in banda tuti do.
E tuti do, sora del só cliché,
Checo, travers tresento ani
donse 'na man 'fa do veci conpari,
'fa do furbi sensèri;
pò 'ndon pa' i nostri afari.
E s'ciao (dison, si qualchidun ne scolta)

Qua ò vist "Il Galateo in Bosco"
andar driocul, girar e far la òlta.

ora e semidistrutto
e pallido come sembra,
lasciamolo stare, fidiamoci
di lui—e di chi verrà
(non è così che un canto va terminato?),
lasciamo che ci lasci da parte tutti e due.
E tutti e due, di sopra il suo cliché,
Cecco, attraverso trecento anni
diamoci una mano come due vecchi compari,
come due furbi sensali;
andiamo poi per i fatti nostri.
E amen (diciamo, se qualcuno ci ascolta).

Qui ho visto "Il Galateo in Bosco"
indietreggiare, girare e capitombolar via.

now and half destroyed
and pallid as it seems,
let's leave it alone, let's trust
in it—and in those who will follow us
(isn't this the way a song ends?),
let's allow it to leave us both aside.
And let's both of us, over its cliché,
Cecco, across three hundred years
let's shake hands like two old cronies,
like two wily middlemen;
then let's go our own ways.
And amen (let's say, in case anyone is listening).

Here I saw *Il Galateo in Bosco*
fall back, turn and tumble away headlong.

MISTIERÒI

Come élo che posse 'ver corajo
de ciamarve qua, de farve segno co la man.
'Na man che no l'é pi de la só onbría
cagnina e caía,
anzhi 'na sgrifa, ma tèndra 'fa molena.
Epuro ades calcossa la tien sú,
no so se 'n sgranf o se 'na forzha;
par quel che l'é, la é tuta vostra,
e voi dèghe l' polso par ciamarve.
Dèghe 'na pena che no la se schinche,
fè che la ponta sul sfój no la se inciónpe.
Me par de no 'ver gnent da méter-dó
par scuminzhiar 'sto telex
che tut al gnent bisogna che 'l traverse
(tut al gran seramènt
che 'l brusa come solfer
che l'incaróla e l'intrunis).
Ma proarò la trazha, almanco, de 'n amor—
fora par là inte 'l scur
orbo dei pra del passà.
Cussì
. . . .
[ ]

PICCOLI, POVERI MESTIERI

Come posso aver coraggio
di chiamarvi qui, di farvi cenno con la mano.
Una mano che non è più della sua ombra
gretta ed avara,
anzi una grinfia, ma tenera come mollica.
Eppure qualcosa adesso la sostiene,
non so se un crampo o una forza;
per quel che vale, è tutta vostra,
e voi datele la forza di chiamarvi.
Datele una penna che non si torca,
fate che la punta sul foglio non inciampi.
Mi pare di non aver nulla da buttar giù
per dare inizio a questo telex
che tutto il nulla deve attraversare
(la bruciante strettoia
che come zolfo brucia
che corrode e intontisce).
Ma tenterò la traccia, almeno, di un amore—
fuori di là nel buio
pesto dei prati del passato.
Così
. . . .
[ ]

SMALL AND HUMBLE OCCUPATIONS

How shall I find the courage
to summon you here, to beckon to you with my hand.
A hand divorced from its shadow,
greedy and mean,
a claw, rather, but soft as breadcrumbs.
And yet something holds it up now,
I don't know if it's a cramp or a force;
for whatever it's worth, it's all yours,
give it the power to summon you.
Give it a pen that won't bend,
don't let the point catch on the page.
I seem to have nothing to put down
to start this telex
that must cross the whole void
(the blazing passageway
that burns like sulfur
that corrodes and stuns).
But I will try for a trace, at least, of a love—
outside there in the pitch dark
of long-ago meadows.
And so
. . . .
[   ]

Cussì, sote 'l camin squasi stusà
se 'n tosatèl vardéa
par quela finestrela cèa
che su la sera la féa 'ncora lustro
in medo ala fulisca
(ah che bel blu, che arjento,
che grísoi de l'inverno inbarlumidi
de ciaro e neve inte la finestrela):
che èrelo, pò, che passéa, che batéa
su quel viero, e sparía
no so se zhotegando o se 'nte 'n bal;
èreli tuti lori, none, del vostro tènp,
cola só fan de radici la só sé
de vin pìzhol, cole só fadighe che
le ghe 'vea ingropá tuta la figura
fin squasi a canbiarghe natura?
Ma co mi, tosatèl, quant maturloni
e quant de bona vója, senpre, e boni . . .
E mi i vede, me par, farme 'n póch marameo,
zhignarme, ridolar, pò farme ciao . . .
. . . .

Così, sotto il camino quasi spento,
se un ragazzetto guardava
attraverso quella minuscola finestra
che chiara appariva ancora sotto sera
in mezzo alla fuliggine
(ah che bel blu, che argento,
che brividi d'inverno abbacinanti
di neve e luce nella finestrella):
chi era mai che passava, che batteva
su quel vetro, e spariva
non so se zoppicando oppur danzando;
erano tutti loro, nonne, quelli del vostro tempo
con la loro fame di radicchi, con la sete
di vinello, con le fatiche che
avevano contorto loro tutta la figura
fino a modificarne quasi la natura?
Ma con me, ragazzetto, che mattacchioni,
e quanto di buon umore e sempre buoni . . .
E li vedo, mi pare, far marameo,
ammiccarmi, ridere sottilmente, poi farmi ciao . . .
. . . .

And so, under the nearly extinguished fireplace
if a small boy were looking
through that tiny window
that still appeared clear in the evening
in the middle of the grime
(oh what lovely blue, what silver,
what dazzling winter chills
of light and snow in the small window):
whoever could it have been that passed, that rapped
on the windowpane, and disappeared
limping or dancing I don't know;
were they all people from your day, grandmothers,
with their hunger for wild chicory,
their thirst for young wine,
with the labors that twisted their shapes
and almost changed their natures?
But with me, a little boy, what scatterbrains,
how merry they always were and how good . . .
I seem to see them now, thumbing their noses at me,
winking at me, laughing softly, then saying "so long" . . .
. . . .

Menadas

Strassinar la mussa:
par che la slíssole sora 'l blu del jazh
e invezhe, co 'sto mazh
co 'sto grun de taje che l'à ados,
la se infonda, o la ne scanpa
e la ris'cia de ciaparne sote,
de trarne dó pa' i bus, dó par i fos.
Forzha mus, cola mussa, e sú 'l mostazh!

Trasportatori di tronchi

Trascinare la slitta:
sembra che scivoli sopra l'azzurro del ghiaccio
e invece, con questo mazzo
con questo mucchio che la sovrasta di tronchi,
affonda, o sfugge
e rischia di venirci addosso,
di spingerci giù per i burroni, giù per i fossi.
Forza asino, con la slitta, e su la fronte!

Log Haulers

Pull that sledge:
it seems to slip over the blue of the ice
and instead, with this load
this heap of logs that overflows it
it's sinking, it's getting away,
it threatens to fall on us,
knocking us down into the gullies, into the ditches.
Come on, donkey, with that sledge. Hold your head high!

Carer

Al carèr ve fa i car
ben tressadi e siguri
cole rode che sguinzha-sú 'l paltan
cole rode che salta su la piera
e coi zhercion de fero che i tien duri . . .
Passa, car, par portarne a laorar,
passa, car, co noaltri sora 'l mar
se qua no ne basta pi la tera . . .

Carraio

Il carraio vi fa i carri
ben costruiti e sicuri
con le ruote che spruzzano fango
con le ruote che saltano sui sassi
e con i cerchioni di ferro che stan saldi . . .
Passa, carro, per portarci a lavorare,
passa, carro, con noi sopra il mare
se qua la terra più non ci basta . . .

Wheelwright

The wheelwright makes you wagons
well-built and sturdy
with wheels that splatter mud
with wheels that bounce over stones
and iron rims that hold fast . . .
Get along, wagon, and take us to work.
Get along with us, wagon, over the sea,
if here the land no longer supplies our needs . . .

Pastor

I pastor, che 'na òlta i ghe ciaméa
"pastre" e che i val in poesia
de pi de ogn'altra categoria
parché in Arcadia lori i comandéa,
i pararàe bestie, se un li vede
inpetoladi senpre intra le fede
le càvere i can e i cavai.
E no l'é vera: òmi i resta e poeti
e re de Arcadie che gnessun
savarà mai.

Pastori

I pastori, che una volta eran detti
"pastre" e che contano in poesia
più d'ogni altra categoria
perché in Arcadia loro comandavano,
sembrerebbero bestie, a chi li veda
impiastricciati sempre tra le agnelle
le capre i cani ed i cavalli.
E non è vero: uomini restano e poeti
e re di Arcadie che nessuno
saprà mai.

Herdsmen

Herdsmen, who once were called
sheep herders and who occupy more space in poetry
than any other category
because in Arcadia they ruled,
would seem like animals to someone
who always sees them mud-smeared among the ewes
goats dogs and horses.
It's not true: they're still men and poets
and kings of Arcadias
no one will ever know.

Marascalco

Al fa senpre 'n poca de paura
'l marascalco inte la só botega
cussì fonda de fóghi e cussì scura;
ma soratut l'é par lu che se próa
paura, quande che i feri che i bróa
al ghe incioda a le zhate
de mus cavai e mui:
che sul mostazh no ghe rive 'na panéta
de colpo, quela che da senpre
inte 'l viver, dal viver, ne spèta.

Maniscalco

Ci fa sempre un po' di paura
il maniscalco nella sua bottega
così fonda di fuochi e così buia;
ma è per lui soprattutto
che si teme, quando i ferri roventi
inchioda alle zampe
di asini cavalli e muli:
che gli capiti sul grugno un calcio secco
lo stesso che vivendo
dal vivere, da sempre, ci aspetta.

Blacksmith

He always frightens us a bit
the blacksmith in his smithy
so full of fire, so dark;
but it's for him above all
that we fear when he nails
the red-hot iron onto the hooves
of donkeys, horses, and mules:
we're afraid he might
get kicked right in the face,
the very thing, that just by living,
we've always expected.

Justaonbrele

Se justa onbrele: pò va
che no 'l pióf mai che basta
parché se posse inpignirse la panzha.
Ma che man che ghe vól,
che soramànego che zhata,
par far un onbrelin squasi da sposa
de 'na onbrelata vecia e meda in tòch:
e ve pàrelo póch?

Ombrellaio

S'aggiustano ombrelli:
poi, sta' a vedere!
mai piove abbastanza
che ci si possa riempire la pancia!
Ma che mano ci vuole,
che abilità che tocco (zampa)
per fare un ombrellino quasi da sposa
d'un ombrellaccio vecchio e sbrindellato:
e vi par poco?

Umbrella Man

They mend umbrellas:
then see what happens!
it never rains enough
to fill their bellies.
But what a hand, what skill
what deftness it takes to make
a nice little umbrella—
almost fit for a bride—
from an ugly, old and tattered one:
you think that's easily done?

Calierer, bandeta

Che feste squasi de zhechin e de ori
no sali far, bandéta e calierèri!
Al ran e 'l stagno i boje intra de lori,
cola le jozhe che tut justa e péta:
anca 'ste póre tece, ste póre
inprestiòle che par laorar ne ocore
e par farse un s'ciant da magnar.
Brao, stagnin, vienme a catar!

Calderaio, lattoniere

Che feste quasi di zecchino e di ori
non sanno fare, calderai e lattonieri!
Rame e stagno bollono tra loro,
cadono le gocce che tutto aggiustano e rappezzano:
anche queste povere pentole, questi poveri
arnesi che ci servono per lavorare
e per farci un boccone da mangiare.
Bravo, stagnaro, vienmi a trovare!

Tinkers and Tinsmiths

What jolly jingling of ducats and gold
tinkers and tinsmiths make!
They boil copper and tin
and the drops that fall
mend and patch things together.
Even these dented pans,
these poor common tools
we use in our work
and to cook our food.
Bravo, tinsmith, come to my house!

Moleta

Gusa e gusa,
cussì 'l taja e cussì 'l sbusa
cussì 'l lustra 'sto cortel,
doperèlo col zharvel,
co 'l porzhel sora la tola,
che grìzhol de s'ciantis che fa la mola,
gira e grata grata e gira
'na feta de polenta se la tira.

Arrotino

Arrota e arrota,
così taglia e così fora
così brilla questo coltello,
adoperatelo con cervello,
con il maiale sopra la tavola,
che raccapriccio di scintille fa la mola,
gira e gratta gratta e gira
una fetta di polenta alfin ci arriva.

Knife-Grinder

It grinds and grinds
that's how it cuts
and that's how it pierces,
that's how it shines
this knife of mine,
use it the very best you're able
with the pork roast on the table.
What awful sparks the grindstone makes,
turn and scrape, scrape and turn,
a slice of polenta is all we'll earn.

Conzhacareghe, caregheta

Riva riva i caregheta
che i é cofà 'na società segreta,
i à 'n dèrego che sol che lori i sa
e 'na sior'Ana che sol che lori i sa:
eco 'l primo che 'l passa,
l'inpaja la carega e inte la paja 'l ghe assa
una renga che 'l gat sgrifarà via,
cussì quel che vien dopo, bon colega,
catarà 'na carega
anca lu da inpajar, e così sia.

Impagliatori di seggiole, seggiolai

Arrivano, arrivano i seggiolai
che formano tra loro quasi una società segreta,
usano un gergo che solo loro conoscono
e hanno un vuoto in pancia che loro soli sanno:
ecco il primo che passa,
impaglia la sedia e tra la paglia lascia
un'aringa che il gatto strapperà via,
così chi verrà dopo, buon collega,
troverà una sedia
anche lui da impagliare, e così sia.

Chairmakers, Chairmenders

Here come the chairmakers:
almost a secret society in themselves,
they use a jargon no one else knows,
the gnawing in their bellies grows.
Here's the first one to arrive,
he stuffs the chair and in the straw
leaves a herring for the cat to claw
so the next mender, who's his friend,
will also find a chair to mend,
and so on, without end.

Femene che le fila

Filar co corlo e fus
inte i dì bassi e curti che i mór in filò . . .
Filar par tante ore
che no le vien pagade gnent
parché le femene—se sa—no conta gnent.
Cànevo lana e lin
tele grosse e tele in fin
par tuta la dènt del colmèl:
ore nostre che no le val gnent
gnent cofà le ciàcole a filò . . .

Filatrici

Filare con fuso ed arcolaio
nei giorni bassi e corti che si spengono nelle veglie nelle stalle . . .
Filare per tante ore
che vengono pagate nulla
perché le donne—si sa—non contan nulla.
Canapa, lana e lino
tele grosse e tele di fino
per tutta la gente della contrada:
ore nostre che non valgon nulla,
nulla come le chiacchiere nelle veglie . . .

Spinners

Spinning with wheel and spindle
in the short dark days
that end with vigils in the stables . . .
Spinning for endless hours
for which we're never paid
because—everyone knows—women
aren't worth a thing.
Hemp, wool, and linen
rough weave and fine
for all the people who live nearby:
like the idle evening chatter,
our long hours don't seem to matter . . .

Femene che le lava

Tute le femene le va dó al lavador:
no l'é 'n mistier 'sto qua
ma l'é 'n destin, cofà l'amor
o 'n fiól, o la só ora co la vien.
La va dó l'ora e la lava
co l'acqua che la fila via,
l'acqua che anca de 'sta vita
e no sol de 'ste póche nostre robe
la ne fa pulizhia.

Donne che lavano

Tutte le donne si recano al lavatoio:
non è un lavoro codesto,
è un destino, come l'amore
o un figlio, o come l'ora nostra quando viene.
Va giù l'ora e lava
con l'acqua che fila via,
l'acqua che anche di questa vita
e non solo di questi nostri pochi indumenti
ci fa pulizia.

Washerwomen

All the women go to the wash-house:
this isn't really work,
it's a "destiny," like love,
a child, or the hour when our time is up.
Time passes and washes
with water that trickles away,
the water that cleanses us
not only of our few belongings
but of our very lives.

. . . .

Cussì inocà col cór son restà là
a la finestrela cèa . . .
E svodà pian pianin la se 'véa
e in éla altro che stele no ghe n'era
e 'l libret de le none e dei só tènp se 'véa serà.
. . . .

"Ma, voi, benedisè
ancora 'na òlta 'l vostro nevodet,
parché ades che l'é 'n ón, debòto consumà,
par voaltre 'l mantegne quel che, tosatèl, l'à lodà."

. . . .

Così ammaliato con il cuore sono rimasto là
alla piccola finestra . . .
E la si vedeva svuotarsi piano piano
e in essa non v'erano che stelle
e il libretto delle nonne e dei loro tempi si era chiuso.
. . . .

"Ma, voi, benedite
una volta ancora il vostro nipotino,
perché adesso che è un uomo, quasi consunto,
per voi mantenga quanto, bambino, ha lodato."

. . . .

And so, my heart bewitched, I stayed there
at that tiny window . . .
And I saw it empty itself slowly
until it held only the stars
and the small book of the grandmothers and of their times was closed.
. . . .

"Bless, then, once more, your grandson,
so that, a man now, and almost finished,
he may keep praising, undiminished,
what he praised as a child."

ALTO, ALTRO LINGUAGGIO, FUORI IDIOMA?

Lingue fioriscono affascinano
inselvano e tradiscono in mille
    aghi di mutismi e sordità
sprofondano e aguzzano in tanti e tantissimi idioti
Lingue tra i cui baratri invano
si crede passare—fioriti, fioriti, in altissimi
    sapori e odori, ma sono idiozia
Idioma, non altro, è ciò che mi attraversa
in persecuzioni e aneliti h j k ch ch ch
    idioma
    è quel gesto ingessato
    che accumula
    sere sforbiciate via verso il niente. Ma
pare che da rocks crudelmente franti tra
i denti diamantiferi, in
ebbri liquori vengano gl'idiomi!
Pare, ognuno, residuo di sé, di
io-lingua, ridotto a seduzione!
Ma vedi come—in idioma—corra i più orribili rischi
la stessa nebbia fatata del mondo, stock
di ogni estatico scegliere, di ogni devozione
    E là mi trascino, all'intraducibile perché
    fuori-idioma, al qui, al sùbito,
    al circuito chiuso che pulsa,

HIGH, OTHER DICTION, BEYOND IDIOM?

Languages flourish fascinate
take to the woods and betray in a thousand
    needles of silence and deafness
they founder and are whetted in so very many idiots
Languages among whose abysses in vain
we think we pass—flowering, flowering, in the highest
    savours and scents, but they're idiocy
Idiom, nothing else, is what passes through me
in persecutions and gasps h j k ch ch ch
    idiom
    is that gesture set in plaster
    that accumulates
    evenings scissored away toward nothingness. But
it seems that from rocks cruelly shattered between
diamond-bearing teeth, in
drunken liquors idioms come!
Each seems the residue of itself, of
me-language, reduced to seduction!
But see how—in idiom—the same enchanted
mist of the world runs the most horrible risks, stock
of every ecstatic choice, every devotion
    And I drag myself there, to the untranslatable why
    beyond-idiom, to the here and now,
    to the pulsating closed circuit,

al grumo, al giro di guizzi in un monitor
Non vi siano idiomi, né traduzioni, ora
entro il disperso
il multivirato sperperarsi in sé
di questo ritornante attacco dell'autunno.
"Attacco," "traduzioni," che dissi? O
altri sinonimi h j k ch ch ch
sempre più nervosamente adatti, in altri idiomi?
Ma che m'interessa ormai degli idiomi?
Ma sì, invece, di qualche
piccola poesia, che non vorrebbe saperne
ma pur vive e muore in essi—di ciò m'interessa
e del foglio di carta
per sempre rapinato dall'oscurità
ventosa di una ValPiave
davvero definitivamente
canadese o australiana
o chi sa.

to the clot, to the flashes rotating in a monitor
Let there be no idioms, or translations, now
within the scattered
the multi-toned squandering in itself
of this recurring onset of autumn.
"Onset," "translations," what did I say? Or
other synonyms h j k ch ch ch
always more nervously adapted, in other idioms?
But what do I care about idioms now?
Yes, I do care, rather, about some
small poem, that wouldn't want to deal with it
but yet lives and dies in idioms—*that* I do care about
and about the sheet of paper
carried off forever from the gusty
darkness of a Piave Valley
truly definitively
Canadian or Australian
or who knows what.

I

Docile e qua e là riluttante assai
feudo di Nino—ti mantieni
con la tua stessa immensità
con la tua stessa intensità
per tante valli e dossi posati qui in te
da chissà quante e quali eternità.
Mi sorridono le tue vertigini
m'accarezzano i buffi dei tuoi rovi
che sono i fior-fiori dell'invernale universo,
un che di brina spuma e ore
cui non spetta, nemmeno lontanamente, morire—
segno di, in mille e mille respiri, preservare
e regno di—alitando—sopravanzare—

Feudo che emani emani emani
da te, che esprimi accogli
e nascondi
ma soprattutto spalanchi te e noi
e ciò che mai
potrà essere in noi
ma che è qui, se-lo-vuoi,
sterpo betulla croco
culla di dovizia primizia e foco

Docile, Reluctant

I

Docile and, here and there, very reluctant
Nino's fiefdom—you maintain yourself
with your same immensity
your very same intensity
through so many valleys and hilltops placed here in you
from who knows how many and which eternities.
Your dizzying heights smile at me
I'm caressed by the puffs of your brambles
that are the flower-flowers of the winter universe,
a bit of hoar-frost foam and hours
which one doesn't expect, not even remotely, to die—
            sign of, in thousands and thousands of breaths, preserving
and realm of—panting—overcoming—

    Fiefdom that you emanate emanate emanate
    from yourself, that you express gather together
    and hide
    but above all you lay open yourself and us
    and that which can never
    be in us
    but is here, should-you-wish-it,
    dry branch, birch tree, crocus,
    cradle of plenty, first fruits and focus

applicato da uccelli d'ogni più preziosa estrazione
Silenzio troppo poco umano così
che dà, per scale di confronti ciò
che è umano—e che sta nell'amore, amerà

2

Nessuna tristezza per i me stessi
che non vi ho ritrovati
né per gli altri, i cari amici, che sempre ho ritrovati,
anche se talvolta più vaghi,
più paghi
degli ultimi arboscelli nei fondi o sui crinali—
Nulla che parli davvero
di cose effimere o finali
bensì della pertinenza,
bensì del fatto, della mai
mai fattuale presenza,
che pur qui si dà giustamente straripando
da tutti gli altrove e singolarità
alla nostra quasi-indolenza
Quanto quanto qui distilla
e si distillò quale paradiso
perfino dolorosamente nel suo insistere muto
ora è soltanto lieto, e non distrattamente,

applied by birds of every most precious extraction
    Silence too little human so that
    it gives, through steps of confrontations, that
    which is human—and that remains in love, it will love

2

No sadness for those selves of mine
which I have not found
nor for the others, the dear friends, whom I have always found again,
though sometimes less intent,
more content
with the last twigs in the depths or on the crests—
Nothing that really speaks
about fleeting or final things
but about the relevance,
but about the fact, of the never
ever factual presence,
that even here gives itself rightly overflowing
from all the elsewheres and singularities
        to our near-indolence
How very much distills here
and was distilled as paradise
downright sadly in its mute insistence
and is now only happy, not distractedly,

ma i suoi valori li compie e li ritira
e li riacconsente un posto più in là
comodi e umili anche se dalle nostre mani
alquanto strani e stralontani
E nei grigiori assopiti, appena specchianti
con gridii di dipinte piume e sbeccuzzati silenzi
(è) come se noi e i nostri ricordi
ma più i nostri presenti
si unissero senza appello, ma non sotto imperio,
ma induzioni di ragionamenti
che non lo saranno mai più, per aver raggiunto
pacatamente (e insegnandolo) gli elementi

but it achieves its values and withdraws them
and again grants them a place farther on,
useful and humble even if from our hands
somewhat strange and very far off
And in the drowsy darkness, scarcely mirroring
with cries of painted plumes and debeaked silences
(it is) as though we and our memories
but even more our here and nows
were to unite without appeal, but not under compulsion,
but inductions of reasonings
that will never be such again, because they have peacefully
reached (and by teaching reasoning) the elements

New Poems

Argentini grovigli dei tuoi percorsi

(per Pasolini, 1975–1995)
Fora par al Furlàn

E ora—forse—mai—
sei nel farsi e disfarsi
di prati pensieri spini arsi
        d'azzurro, attimo ad attimo,
                dai piani a montani primordi
Non c'è nulla che valga
ad esaurire questa inimmaginabile
                                vibratilità
né mano che entri decidendo
un senso ultimativo
—come a un fossile film—alla tua vita

o Benandante

Quasi a tentoni e semiorbi ma quasi
lieti incrociamo di già
gli argentini grovigli dei tuoi percorsi
verso altri raccolti
        altri   elementi
. . . .

Silvery Tangles of Your Wanderings

(for Pasolini, 1975–1995)
Crossing Friuli

And now—perhaps—never—
you exist in the making and unmaking
of burnt meadows thoughts thorns
        of azure, moment by moment,
                from the plains to primordial peaks
There is nothing that merits
exhausting this unimaginable
                                vibratility
nor hand that enters into deciding
a definitive meaning
—as with a fossilized film—to your life

oh Wandering Spirit

Almost groping and halfblind but almost
joyful we already cross
the silvery tangles of your wanderings
toward other harvests
        other   elements
. . . .

In ciascuna di queste

In ciascuna di queste
case si
continua certo a nascere
con gioia appena movente
con lavoro accanito ma dolce

Ora nella folta compresenza
nel rilassarsi del verde in altri verdi
tutto è preparato a
piante canne fogliami fiumane

Ognuno è sicurissimo di ognuno
anche se non si vedono, se non vi vedo
Ogni stelo o canna o fusto
sprona ad essergli simile, dedito
ad ogni accoglienza, senza
parole d'ordine allucinazioni
d'ordini-eccessi
—Non si esaurisce
—È troppo verde in atto
—È troppo essere, e dolce
—È forte //   perdita d'essere //
                          sogno sull'essere

In Each of These Houses

In each of these
houses we
continue surely to be born
with barely stirring joy
with labor violent but sweet

Now in the crowded coming together
in the relaxing of the green into other greens
everything is prepared for
plants reeds foliage torrents

Everyone is very sure of everyone
even if they don't see each other, if I don't see you
Every stem or reed or stalk
spurs each to resemble the other, dedicated
to every acceptance, without
passwords hallucinations
of orders-excesses
—It doesn't exhaust itself
—It's too green in motion
—It's too much being, and sweet
—It's strong // loss of being //
dream about being

Ticchettio

dopo l'esplosione della centrale atomica di Cernobyl

Tenui-cupi dolori in sé fece nascere e poi
soffocò, seppellì nel suo procedere d'oro
    quest'infinita, senza tregua, estate
Non sono ammesse altre ragioni che l'oro
nel suo stato più innaturalmente evidente
Non sono ammessi altri dèi che la sua
    incontinente innocenza che sottili barbarie
    di siccità quasi immaginarie
    trascina seco in varii avanti, impentiti,
    in una sola istanza che si regge sull'
    orlo di ogni legge, si protegge
    nel suo stesso inventarsi di cometa
    nel suo farsi strascico in polveri di seta
    nel suo coinvolgere ma
    in sempre più svolgente, svolgentesi amistà
    nel fare intimo ogni beato estraniamento
    nel suo—che tutto lascia ai lati—
    impennato, secreto   mutamento

*

Ticking (Like a Geiger Counter)

After the Explosion at the Chernobyl Nuclear Center

It caused tenuous-dark pains in itself to be born and then
suffocated, buried in its golden proceeding
    this endless, relentless summer
No other reasons are admitted except gold
in its most unnaturally evident state
No other gods are admitted except its
    incontinent innocence that drags with it
    subtle barbarisms
    of almost imaginary drought
    in various advances, impenitent,
    in a single instance that stands on the
    edge of every law, protects itself
    in its very self-invention as comet
    in making itself into a trail of dust powders
    in its involving but
    always more developing, happening amity
    in making intimate every blessed estrangement
    in its—that leaves everything aside—
    rearing, secret   change

*

Voglia semplice, fregola gentile e
acquiescente di miriadi d'insetti d'oro
          locuste o anche roditori
     o ricci e grilli in lavorio—
     al di là d'ogni provenienza
     al di là d'ogni sospetto
          questa infinita—senza tregua—estate
     Quanto mai fu ritenuto possibile si confà
     strusciando strisciando strascinando
     all'idea stessa di possibilità

*

Estate estate, ch'io ti accompagni nel falso
tuo infinito di eterna/appena-sopravvivente
amistà, siccità di toni e ori e clivi,
mostrali a noi per quel che sono—
nel tuo ticchettio   docilmente radioattivi . . .

(1986–87)

Simple desire, spawning soft and
acquiescent of myriads of golden insects
          locusts or even rodents
     or hedgehogs and hardworking crickets—
     beyond all provenance
     all suspicion
          this endless—relentless—summer
     Whatever was once believed possible fits
     slipping sliding slithering
     the very idea of possibility

*

Summer summer, so that I can accompany you in your
false heaven of eternal/barely-surviving
amity, drought of tones and golds and hillocks,
show them to us for what they are—
in your quietly radioactive   ticking . . .

(1986–87)

Altri papaveri

Dopo Sarejevo

Fieri di una fierezza e foia barbara
sovrabbondanti con ogni petalo
rosso + rosso + rosso + rosso
    coup de dés maledetto
    sanguinose potenze dilaganti,
    quasi ognuno di voi a coprire un prato intero—
da che
da che mondi stragiferi
stragiferi papaveri
        qui vi accampaste avvampando,
        sfacciato forno del rosso
        che in misteriche chiazze
        non cessa di accedere sgorgar su
        straventando i soliti maggi grigioblù?

Come i calabroni si fanno sempre più enormi
        CRABRO CRABRO
e quasi difformi da ogni destino
e le limacce budella a stravento su verzure:
via! via! è tempo di toglier via questa primavera
di pozze di sangue da tiri da cecchino
Correre Correre

Other Poppies

After Sarajevo

Fierce with a fierceness barbaric and rutting
overflowing with every petal
red + red + red + red
cursed throw of the dice
bloody powers spreading,
as though each of you covered a whole meadow—
from what
from what slaughtering worlds
slaughtering poppies
did you settle here blazing,
brazen furnace of red
that in cultish splatters
never stops drawing near welling up
overblowing the usual greyblue Mays?

As the giant hornets grow increasingly huge
CRABRO CRABRO
and almost unlike any destiny
and slimy guts blown over greenery:
flee! flee! It's time to end this spring
of pools of blood from sniper fire
Run Run

coprendosi in affanno teste e braccia e corpi orbi
correre correre per chi
corre e corre sotto calabroni e cecchini
e in orridi papaveri finì

(incerti frammenti 1993–95)

breathlessly covering your heads and arms and blind bodies
run run for the one
who runs and runs under hornets and snipers
and died among horrible poppies

(uncertain fragments 1993–95)

Notes and Commentary

Filò per il Casanova di Fellini

Letter from Federico Fellini to Andrea Zanzotto

T.N.: Domenico ("Nico") Naldini is a writer and poet as well as the biographer of his cousin, Pier Paolo Pasolini. Naldini directed the documentary film *Fascista!* (1973) and has worked in various capacities in publishing and at the film studios of Cinecittà, including disseminating publicity for the film, Fellini's *Casanova.* It was Naldini who suggested to Fellini that he contact Zanzotto to provide the texts required for the film.

"London Lullaby"

T.N.: Both the Italian and the English versions of Fellini's *Casanova* contain only a small portion, untranslated, of the original text of "London Lullaby" written by Zanzotto. The text published here represents Zanzotto's composition in its entirety. At the request of Nino Rota, who composed the music for the film, the poet also provided the shorter version adapted in both versions of the film. Rota's musical accompaniment to "London Lullaby" furnishes a leitmotif—sad, plaintive, haunting—that is associated first with the women embroidering a large white garment, the craftswomen, or *inpiraresse,* mentioned in the poem, and later with the giant woman from the Veneto who, due to an unfortunate marriage, has become a character in a London circus. Encouraged by her two dwarf attendants to "sing us a song of your city," the giantess, in her bath, sings the initial lines from the opening stanzas, along with the refrain. Casanova, played by Donald Sutherland in the film, observes the woman in the tub with the dwarfs.

"Peasants Wake"

T.N.: Zanzotto himself suggested the title "Peasants Wake" for this English-language version of "Filò," and his choice merits comment. James Joyce's *Finnegans Wake,* first published in 1939, is a densely complex work drawing on many languages. Joyce makes use of a wide variety of puns, counting rhymes, and nonsense words in creating cyclical patterns of death and resurrection. The title itself stands as a fitting emblem for Joyce's brilliantly obscure prose, which contains passages of unforgettable humor and great lyrical beauty. For example, the proper noun "Finnegan" turns back upon itself suggesting the "end" (*fine* in Italian) "again," imitating, in the process, life's eternal cycle of decay and resurgence. The title's justly famous missing apostrophe and the lack of other punctuation also create rich ambiguities. The reader is presented with various possibilities that appear simultaneously: should the first word be read as a possessive adjective in the singular or the plural? The word "wake" is equally ambiguous as it can be read both as a noun and a verb: i.e., the imperative, "Finnegans Wake!," or the noun, "The Wake of the Finnegans."

Having lived in Trieste before World War I, Joyce possessed a deep knowledge of Italian and reportedly spoke it at home with Nora Barnacle, the woman with whom he shared his life, and their two children, Lucia and Giorgio Joyce. In addition to writing a series of literary articles for the *Piccolo della Sera,* the Trieste newspaper, Joyce himself "translated" or recreated, we might say, a portion of *Finnegans Wake* in Italian: *Anna Livia Pluribelle.*

Idioma

"Idioma" (Idiom) is to be understood according to every etymological diffraction and beyond, from the fullness of nascent, incoercible speech as an entirely unique blossoming to the opposite pole of closure in the peculiarity by which we arrive at the heading "idiocy." Language, private language, fact private and depriving; an excess of privacy and therefore of closure-privation-deprivation. An emphasis on peculiarity: but also, on the contrary, a linguistic means understood completely as an overflowing from that peculiarity.

T.N.: Zanzotto often makes use of terms from linguistics, and his poetry touches on the mystery of human speech itself. His note on "idiom" reminds us that dialect remains irrepressibly alive, always in the process of being born or recreated. Yet, at the same time, dialect is also limited in its range of diffusion and considered inferior. At the furthest extreme, a totally private language would isolate a person, depriving him or her of the ability to communicate.

"Peoples"

Unfortunately this poem refers to situations that are now unstable.

"Spheres"

"Phosphenes": vortices of signs and luminuous points that are seen keeping the eyes closed (and rubbing them) or also in pathological situations.

"Acouphenes": whistling noises in the ears, also in pathological situations.

"Horizons"

"Oh parents": and parents of parents ad infinitum.

"Special effects": in the cinematic sense.

"I Would Like to Know"

The wall with the writing on it disappeared a long time ago, as did the person referred to.

T.N.: "Nene dictatrice in hoc vico, MCMXXXIX" (to Nene, dictator in this quarter, MCMXXXIX).

"Nino in the Eighties"

The poem refers to an earlier poem, "The Prophecies of Nino," from Zanzotto's collection *La Beltà* (Beauty, 1968) and is, actually, an updating. At that time (in the Sixties) Nino pedaled "between his seventies and his eighties almost flighty."

T.N.: Nino Mura, a handsome, sturdy old peasant, was greatly esteemed by Zanzotto. He represented a vanishing breed, a treasury of peasant lore, in tune with nature, and wise in ancient ways and knowledge regarding phases of the moon and when certain crops should be planted. A decorated hero of both world wars, he was honored by the townspeople on commemorative occasions. He had calling cards printed for himself on which he listed his decorations, called himself "poet" (the card says that he was crowned with laurel by the poet Giovanni Comisso) and peasant, and attributed to himself the following capabilities: actor, astronomer, gastronome, farmer, empiricist, herbalist, and seer. At ninety he still rode his bicycle to Pieve di Soligo every day from his hilltop farm.

"Going Out to Sew"

"Zauberkraft": "magical force," a comfort to Hegel.

"Cavalier": today the raising and cultivation of silkworms are experiencing a rebirth in new and brilliant forms.

"An ample valley shaped like a U": a technical expression from geology. The U-shaped profile is typical of valleys of glacial origin (those of fluvial origin, on the other hand, are characterized by a profile in a V).

"Graphemes": a linguistic term. In homology with "phonemes," considered indivisible units of the sound chain, graphemes are the smallest units of writing that cannot be divided. In a wider sense, the word stands for the written trace of speech.

"Where Are They?"

Onde éli: "Where Are They?": the dialect translation of the famous topos and theme: "ubi sunt." *T.N.:* Although the English-language reader when approaching this series of strophes, which form an extended movement, will no doubt recall the villagers of Edgar Lee Masters's *Spoon River Anthology,* Zanzotto draws upon a medieval European tradition of Latin verse involving the passage of time and people who have gone before us.

T.N.: In the segment "Where Are Tony and Annina," *Pasque* (Easters) refers to a book of poetry published by Zanzotto in 1973.

"For Eugenio Montale on His Eightieth Birthday"

T.N.: Eugenio Montale (1896–1981) is one of the masters of modern poetry and the greatest Italian poet since Leopardi. His three major collections of verse—*Ossi di seppia* (Cuttlefish Bones, 1925), *Le occasioni* (The Occasions, 1939), and *La bufera e altro* (The Storm and Other Things, 1956)—have been widely translated into English, most recently by William Arrowsmith, Dana Gioia, and Jonathan Galassi. Winner of the Nobel Prize for Literature in 1975, Montale was known as "Eusebius" to his friends.

"In Memory of Pasolini"

T.N.: Pier Paolo Pasolini (1922–75), poet, novelist, filmmaker, and political gadfly, perhaps the most important cultural figure in postwar Italy, was murdered in obscure circumstances near Rome in November 1975. Known in the English-speaking world primarily for such films as *The Gospel According to St. Matthew, The Decameron,* and *Salò, or the One Hundred and Twenty Days of Sodom,* Pasolini was instrumental in the contemporary rediscovery of the Italian dialects as vehicles for poetic expression. In addition to his poetic masterpiece in Italian, *Le ceneri di Gramsci* (The Ashes of Gramsci, 1957), his books containing his Friulian dialect poetry, *La meglio gioventù* (The Best Youth, 1954) and *La nuova gioventù* (The New Youth, 1974), have been largely responsible for leading the contemporary revival of writing poetry in the dialects, a phenomenon known as "*la poesia neodialettale*" (new dialect poetry).

Before moving in 1950 to Rome, where he gradually gained fame as a poet, novelist, and filmmaker, Pasolini spent a number of years from the middle to the late 1940s teaching Latin and Italian in rural schools in Friuli, his mother's native region. Zanzotto, himself an active educator throughout his adult life, first became aware of Pasolini through his renown as a teacher. Although Zanzotto taught in a neighboring district of the Veneto, the region bordering Friuli on the west, both young men had the same administrator, who often sang the praises of Pasolini's ingenious teaching methods.

T.N.: The phrase "*alba pratalia*" (literally, "white meadows," translated here as "white expanses of snow") stems from one of the oldest extant examples of written Italian in its evolution from Vulgar Latin: the "Veronese riddle," which dates from the late eighth or early ninth century. The phrase, which also symbolizes the whiteness of a blank sheet of paper, takes on added significance in Zanzotto's poem because Pasolini, who had a deep love for Romance philology and edited two important anthologies of Italian dialect poetry, himself uses "*alba pratalia*" in one of his poems.

"When Toti Died"

Toti Dal Monte was a *soprano leggero* who, with her unique voice, personified a great moment of Italian lyric opera, and who triumphed all over the world in the period between the two world wars. She originated in the area described here, where she spent a great deal of time and was beloved by the people of the Veneto.

"Charlie Chaplin and Gigetto"

Charles Chaplin died on Christmas night 1977.

Dhà che gnessun resta qua par semenzha: "since nobody lives forever" is a popular saying. "Monsieur Verdoux": perhaps the most ambiguous, disturbing, and yet necessary character interpreted by Chaplin. *Note:* There is a reference at the end of this poem to an actual event, the vandalizing of Chaplin's grave in search of nonexistent treasure.

T.N.: decalcomania: "the art or process of transferring pictures or designs from specially designed paper to wood, metal, glass, etc." (*Random House Dictionary,* 2d ed., hereafter *RHD*). Decalcomania also refers to the inexpensive decals that children of the poet's generation, both in Europe and in the United States, would purchase and then transfer to the back of the hand.

T.N.: in Kirlian: "a photographic process that supposedly records electrical discharges naturally emanating from living objects, producing an auralike glow surrounding the object on a photographic plate or film with which the object is in direct contact" (*RHD*).

"And Amen"

"*E amen, e pazienza, e buona notte.*" "And amen, and patience, and good night."

"*Checho*": Cecco Ceccogiato (Nicolò Zotti), a seventeenth-century poet in the dialect of Padua, sang the praises of the beauties of the Montello forest. He is mentioned in the book *Il Galateo in Bosco* (The Book of Forest Manners, 1978), to which this poem bids farewell.

"*Anguane*": nymphs-witches-fairies.

"*Bau-sète, nati-nati, bissi-bissi*": words almost in an infantile idiolect, always to suggest the appearing and disappearing of something, spoken, however, by an adult in order to instill in the child a brief fear that is dispelled by a laugh.

"*I putèi del Mulineto*": "The Children of the Molinetto" is an old local satirical ditty.

"*Queimada brasilèira*": the Brazilian Quiemada was a great burning of forests done to strip the land clean and cultivate it. This was known to the great horde of people from the upper Veneto who emigrated to Brazil at the end of the last century. The Montello forest was felled in great measure to use the land for farming, for supposed social purposes.

"*Magagnò*": a master of the Paduan tongue.

"*a Mantel*": this is the way the old people referred to the Montello forest, perhaps suggesting a mantle or cloak.

"Small and Humble Occupations"

Dedicated to the dear and venerated memory of Angela Bertazzon and Marina Bon. Many times published in plaquettes, this composition was actually conceived as an integral part of the volume *Idioma.* It is also a tribute to the series of woodcuts, *Le arti che vanno per via,* by G. Zompini, with a verse commentary by Questini, published in Venice, 1785.

"*Ma, voi, benedisè . . .*": "But, bless then . . .": a paraphrase of the last two verses of Hölderlin's "To My Venerated Grandmother."

T.N.: Mentioned in the poem "Herdsmen," Arcadia derives its name from the bleak, mountainous region in the Peloponnese. Celebrated by Virgil in his *Eclogues,* it became the traditional, idealized world of the pastoral, a literary genre that has lasted two thousand years, centered around a fictionalized imitation of rural life usually set in a Golden Age. Jacopo Sannazaro published a series of eclogues with the title *Arcadia* circa 1504, which treats the laments, loves, and other activities of various shepherds and shepherdesses in Arcadia. An immensely popular work, Sannazaro's *Arcadia* was a link between the pastorals of Theocritus, Virgil, and those of Sidney, Spenser, and later writers. Zanzotto himself has written a book, *IX Ecloghe* (IX Eclogues, 1962), in tribute to what he calls "the great shadow of Virgil."

When Zanzotto's dialect poem "Pastor" (Herdsmen) was read over the radio in his locality, the station received numerous enthusiastic calls from shepherds who heard the poem as they tended their flocks. "Variante 1984" is Zanzotto's response to their warm response: a gesture typical of the Arcadian tradition, which features numerous "responsive verses" or "singing matches." "Variante 1984": "Anca adès no i val manco / e cola radiolina al fianco / sote 'l sol o le stele / i scolta le canzhon pi bele" (Today they're still highly prized / with their radios at their sides / under the sun or under the stars / they follow the hit songs on the charts).

"High, Other Diction, Beyond Idiom?"

In the chain connected to "idiom." See the note to "idiom" above.

T.N.: "In persecutions and gasps h j k ch ch ch": recalls Aldo Palazzeschi's poem, "La fontana malata" (The Sick Fountain): "Clof, clop, cloch / cloffete, / cloppete, / clocchete, / chchch . . ."

T.N.: The version of "Alto, altro linguaggio, fuori idioma?" published in this volume varies from the original published in the first Mondadori edition of *Idioma* (1986). Zanzotto decided to change the last line of the original from "o aldilà" (or beyond) to "o chi sa" (or who knows what), as printed here.

New Poems

"Silvery Tangles of Your Wanderings"

In the original, the words "Crossing Friuli" are in Veneto dialect. The *Benandanti* were restless but benign creatures from ancient Friulian folklore, of remote origins.

T.N.: vibratility: "that pertaining to, or of the nature of, vibration" (*RHD*).

T.N.: The hand envisioned in this poem recalls the biblical story of the handwriting on the wall, as in Daniel 5. Zanzotto's image of the "fossilized film" contests a famous theoretical proposition by Pasolini comparing death and film editing.

"Other Poppies"

Crabro is the Latin word for "hornet."

T.N.: From his home in Pieve di Soligo, near Treviso, Zanzotto could hear the planes departing from nearby NATO bases for missions in Bosnia. Italian television broadcast images of snipers in Sarajevo, pools of blood surrounding their victims, amid the flowering of poppies and the appearance of a dangerous species of giant hornet.

Notes on the Author, Editors/Translators, and Artists

Andrea Zanzotto is one of the leading contemporary poets in Europe and the most innovative poetic voice in Italy after Eugenio Montale. A native of the Veneto, he is known for his stylistic inventiveness, his interest in psychoanalysis, and his attempts to find, through language, the origins of myth. In a career that spans five decades and has yielded fourteen books of poetry, Zanzotto's unique achievement bridges the gap between experimentalism and tradition. His works have been translated into various languages and he has been an active literary critic. He was awarded the Feltrinelli Poetry Prize from the Accademia dei Lincei in 1987 and the European Poetry Prize from the city of Münster in 1993.

John P. Welle is Associate Professor of Italian at the University of Notre Dame where he teaches modern Italian literature, film history, and translation studies. The author of *The Poetry of Andrea Zanzotto* and the editor of a volume of essays on film and literature in Italian culture, he has received grants and fellowships from the Fulbright Commission and the National Endowment for the Humanities.

Ruth Feldman has five books of poetry and thirteen previous books of Italian translations to her credit, all poetry with the exception of Primo Levi's concentration camp stories. She has been awarded the John Florio Prize in England, the Circe-Sabaudia in Italy, and the Italo Calvino Prize in the United States. The recipient of a Literary Translator's Fellowship from the National Endowment for the Arts, she has lectured and read at many universities in the United States and Italy. Her poetry has been translated into Italian, French, and Spanish.

Federico Fellini was a cartoonist, journalist, and scriptwriter before beginning his career as a film director. His major films include *La strada, La dolce vita, 8½, Giulietta degli spiriti, Amarcord,* and *Casanova.*

Augusto Murer was an artist active in the Veneto whose monuments to the Resistance movement can be found throughout northern Italy. Acclaimed as one of the greatest modern sculptors in wood, his works are on display at the Augusto Murer Museum in Falcade, Italy.

Illinois Poetry Series ***Laurence Lieberman, Editor***

History Is Your Own Heartbeat
Michael S. Harper (1971)
The Foreclosure
Richard Emil Braun (1972)
The Scrawny Sonnets and Other Narratives
Robert Bagg (1973)
The Creation Frame
Phyllis Thompson (1973)
To All Appearances: Poems New and Selected
Josephine Miles (1974)
The Black Hawk Songs
Michael Borich (1975)
Nightmare Begins Responsibility
Michael S. Harper (1975)
The Wichita Poems
Michael Van Walleghen (1975)
Images of Kin: New and Selected Poems
Michael S. Harper (1977)
Poems of the Two Worlds
Frederick Morgan (1977)
Cumberland Station
Dave Smith (1977)
Tracking
Virginia R. Terris (1977)
Riversongs
Michael Anania (1978)
On Earth as It Is
Dan Masterson (1978)
Coming to Terms
Josephine Miles (1979)
Death Mother and Other Poems
Frederick Morgan (1979)
Goshawk, Antelope
Dave Smith (1979)
Local Men
James Whitehead (1979)
Searching the Drowned Man
Sydney Lea (1980)
With Akhmatova at the Black Gates
Stephen Berg (1981)
Dream Flights
Dave Smith (1981)
More Trouble with the Obvious
Michael Van Walleghen (1981)
The American Book of the Dead
Jim Barnes (1982)
The Floating Candles
Sydney Lea (1982)
Northbook
Frederick Morgan (1982)
Collected Poems, 1930-83
Josephine Miles (1983)
The River Painter
Emily Grosholz (1984)
Healing Song for the Inner Ear
Michael S. Harper (1984)
The Passion of the Right-Angled Man
T. R. Hummer (1984)
Dear John, Dear Coltrane
Michael S. Harper (1985)
Poems from the Sangamon
John Knoepfle (1985)
In It
Stephen Berg (1986)
The Ghosts of Who We Were
Phyllis Thompson (1986)
Moon in a Mason Jar
Robert Wrigley (1986)
Lower-Class Heresy
T. R. Hummer (1987)
Poems: New and Selected
Frederick Morgan (1987)

Furnace Harbor: A Rhapsody of the North Country
Philip D. Church (1988)
Bad Girl, with Hawk
Nance Van Winckel (1988)
Blue Tango
Michael Van Walleghen (1989)
Eden
Dennis Schmitz (1989)
Waiting for Poppa at the Smithtown Diner
Peter Serchuk (1990)
Great Blue
Brendan Galvin (1990)
What My Father Believed
Robert Wrigley (1991)
Something Grazes Our Hair
S. J. Marks (1991)
Walking the Blind Dog
G. E. Murray (1992)
The Sawdust War
Jim Barnes (1992)
The God of Indeterminacy
Sandra McPherson (1993)
Off-Season at the Edge of the World
Debora Greger (1994)
Counting the Black Angels
Len Roberts (1994)
Oblivion
Stephen Berg (1995)
To Us, All Flowers Are Roses
Lorna Goodison (1995)
Honorable Amendments
Michael S. Harper (1995)
Points of Departure
Miller Williams (1995)
Dance Script with Electric Ballerina
Alice Fulton (reissue, 1996)
To the Bone: New and Selected Poems
Sydney Lea (1996)
Floating on Solitude
Dave Smith (3-volume reissue, 1996)
Bruised Paradise
Kevin Stein (1996)
Walt Whitman Bathing
David Wagoner (1996)

National Poetry Series

Eroding Witness
Nathaniel Mackey (1985)
Selected by Michael S. Harper
Palladium
Alice Fulton (1986)
Selected by Mark Strand
Cities in Motion
Sylvia Moss (1987)
Selected by Derek Walcott
The Hand of God and a Few Bright Flowers
William Olsen (1988)
Selected by David Wagoner
The Great Bird of Love
Paul Zimmer (1989)
Selected by William Stafford
Stubborn
Roland Flint (1990)
Selected by Dave Smith

The Surface
Laura Mullen (1991)
Selected by C. K. Williams
The Dig
Lynn Emanuel (1992)
Selected by Gerald Stern
My Alexandria
Mark Doty (1993)
Selected by Philip Levine
The High Road to Taos
Martin Edmunds (1994)
Selected by Donald Hall
Theater of Animals
Samn Stockwell (1995)
Selected by Louise Glück
The Broken World
Marcus Cafagña (1996)
Selected by Yusef Komunyakaa

Other Poetry Volumes

Local Men and *Domains*
James Whitehead (1987)
Her Soul beneath the Bone: Women's Poetry on Breast Cancer
Edited by Leatrice Lifshitz (1988)
Days from a Dream Almanac
Dennis Tedlock (1990)
Working Classics: Poems on Industrial Life
Edited by Peter Oresick and Nicholas Coles (1990)
Hummers, Knucklers, and Slow Curves: Contemporary Baseball Poems
Edited by Don Johnson (1991)
The Double Reckoning of Christopher Columbus
Barbara Helfgott Hyett (1992)
Selected Poems
Jean Garrigue (1992)
New and Selected Poems, 1962-92
Laurence Lieberman (1993)
The Dig and *Hotel Fiesta*
Lynn Emanuel (1994)
For a Living: The Poetry of Work
Edited by Nicholas Coles and Peter Oresick (1995)
The Tracks We Leave: Poems on Endangered Wildlife of North America
Barbara Helfgott Hyett (1996)
Peasants Wake for Fellini's *Casanova* and Other Poems
Andrea Zanzotto; edited and translated by John P. Welle and Ruth Feldman; drawings by Federico Fellini and Augusto Murer (1997)